The Living Tropical Greenhouse

The Living Tropical Greenhouse

Creating a haven for butterflies

John and Maureen Tampion

GUILD OF MASTER CRAFTSMAN PUBLICATIONS LTD

First published 1999 by

Guild of Master Craftsman Publications Ltd,

166 High Street, Lewes, East Sussex BN7 1XU

© GMC Publications Ltd

Text © John and Maureen Tampion 1999

All photographs © Dr J. Tampion: Butterflies Picture Library

ISBN 1 86108 123 5

A catalogue record of this book is available from the British
Library.

Cover design: Rob Wheele at Wheelhouse Design

Book design: Fran Rawlinson

Colour separation by Viscan Graphics (Singapore)

Printed in Hong Kong by H & Y Printing Ltd

10 9 8 7 6 5 4 3 2 1

Acknowledgements

Our first acknowledgements must be to the
butterflies and plants that have inspired this book.
They have lived with us, but may not know us.

There are many in the UK and throughout the
world who have contributed over the years to our
knowledge and experience. Staff at butterfly
houses open to the public are always ready to
help. To mention just a few: Butterfly and
Falconry Park, Long Sutton; Butterfly World,
Stockton-on-Tees; London Butterfly House, Syon
Park; Longleat Butterfly Garden; Stratford-on-
Avon Butterfly Farm; Tropical Butterfly House
and Wildlife Centre, Sheffield.

Of particular mention for their contributions
to breeding tropical butterflies in the UK are
David Lowe, the father of UK butterfly houses;
Clive Farrell whose enthusiasm has carried the
subject forward; Robert Goodden (of Worldwide
Butterflies, Sherborne), a prolific author and
campaigner; Richard Burgess of London Pupae
Supplies; and Paul Batty for his tireless promotion
of the Entomological Livestock Group.

On the plant side, John Vanderplank deserves
special mention for his work with the National
Collection of Passiflora at Kingston Seymor.

No book can be produced without an
excellent editor and we thank Andy Charman and
others at GMC Publications for all their work in
guiding this book to fruition.

Contents

Introduction

A greenhouse is a protected environment in which to grow plants that would not flourish or survive at all in the open air. A tropical greenhouse enables people who live in temperate climates to grow plants that originate in much warmer climates.

When such plants were first introduced into temperate climates, they were kept in structures called hothouses or stove houses that looked like modern-day conservatories. They were a privilege enjoyed only by the very rich, or by those gardeners who looked after them for the rich. The plants themselves were not available to the general public, even if they could have afforded to look after them.

This is no longer the situation, because many tropical plants are available to everyone and most people have at least one or two in their houses as pot plants. With the development of thermostatically controlled heaters and all the modern types of greenhouse or conservatory and other equipment, the structures to house the plants and the facilities to care for them are also readily available. (From this point on, any reference to 'greenhouses' should be taken to include conservatories.)

Our definition of a living tropical greenhouse is one in which no pesticides are used, not even those popularly known as 'natural' or 'organic'. All pests and diseases are controlled by good cultural practices and biological control agents and this enables us to combine together two of the most beautiful creations of nature: plants and butterflies.

This book is about how to create your own miniature 'tropical rainforest', your own tropical

This attractive greenhouse at Abbotsbury Tropical Gardens, Dorset, England, could be run as a living tropical greenhouse.

environment in which you can grow exotic and rarely available plants. Different types of bananas, several of the unusual species of passion flowers, other exotic climbers and many plants that you have probably never heard of before, as well as magnificent specimens of familiar houseplants, can all be yours.

You will be taking the first steps along a path of enlightenment that has no end other than the conservation and enjoyment of plants, butterflies

*The underside of the magnificent tropical Asian swallowtail, the great mormon (*Papilio memnon) *is as colourful as the upperside.*

educate others concerning their world, to help conserve the many species that are threatened by habitat destruction and to gain a fuller understanding of both plants and animals, then we need to breed them ourselves. Only by doing this can we gain that additional knowledge that no photograph, video or article can give. In a world submerged by a deluge of media and virtual reality, we need to touch nature ourselves if we are to discover what is real.

and nature itself. Gardening and the love of plants is so widespread a feature of human life that it needs little encouragement, but extending that love to the creatures that live on plants does. For many gardeners, learning to share their plants with butterflies at all stages of their life-cycles may seem hard at first, but it brings its own rewards.

Butterflies are beautiful – of that there is no doubt. Could we imagine Heaven, Paradise or Nirvana without them? We use their image to conjure up all manner of pleasant feelings, from nature at its purest and best to the virtues of double glazing. Yet, in truth, most people know very little about the life of the butterfly. We see them flitting from flower to flower in an apparently aimless way, fluttering and dancing as they go. We even use this particular image to criticize those who do not give their full attention to the task in hand. In fact, nothing could be further from the truth. The life of a butterfly, in all its fascinating forms and subtleties is as purposeful as that of any human.

If we want to learn about butterflies, to

Of the 20,000 or so species of butterflies that are known, the majority live in tropical climates. We do not know exactly how many species there are because some are undoubtedly still to be discovered. Quite a few of those that have been given scientific names are known mostly from dead adult specimens in the great museums. Their eggs (ova), caterpillars (larvae) and chrysalids (pupae) may not have been seen, and the foodplants on which the ova are laid and the larvae feed may not have been found and identified. For plants, we have a multitude of living collections and societies where they can be studied, grown and the species and cultivars conserved, and there are countless numbers of people with the necessary skills to do this work. This is not the case with most butterflies.

Fortunately, we have a great deal of information on the butterflies of most temperate, developed countries. All stages of the life-cycle have been described and illustrated many times. Many books exist giving details of them, and the usual and unusual larval foodplants have been listed. Habitat destruction may threaten some and climate change others, but their conservation, even if not yet perfect, does receive considerable attention. Many carefully tended reserves have been established and there are books which give practical advice on such matters.

It is very doubtful, however, that all the changes that are necessary will ever be made for the conservation of butterflies outside of reserves. It is unlikely that intensification of agriculture or the use of pesticides will be abandoned, nor will various other important changes in land management and use be adopted. The trend may be for less persistent and more specific pesticides, but we also need to consider the recent advances in genetic engineering, whereby plants are being modified to produce alien substances that are toxic to butterfly larvae. Butterflies now common in cultivated areas are likely to be severely threatened by such 'advances'.

The situation with regard to the butterflies of the tropical regions is much less satisfactory than that of those in temperate zones. A few of the species considered to be so rare that they are in danger of becoming extinct have been protected by international laws. But at the same time, the natural habitats of the butterflies are being destroyed, legally, illegally and sometimes by natural or partially natural disasters, such as the huge forest fires in tropical regions that range over enormous areas. Control measures for 'pest species' spill over to kill other species and there is virtually no effort being made to conserve species which are common today but which may be threatened by the climate changes we are being told to expect.

The pressures from expanding human populations, for both living space and resources, are bound to result in the loss of butterfly habitats. Those concerned with the conservation of vertebrate species have at last realized that breeding in the protected environment of zoos can play a vital role in what is known as 'ex situ conservation strategies'. This lesson has yet to be learnt by many involved with tropical butterfly conservation. It is perhaps unfortunate that in order to obtain funds, many conservationists have had to resort to an emphasis on the direct value of other organisms to humans, by way of providing materials, medicines, knowledge or enjoyment, rather than the preservation of a species for its own intrinsic value.

It might be thought that conserving tropical butterflies is a task that can only be undertaken in tropical climates by persons with a research degree in conservation science. Such a view is entirely erroneous. Firstly, those who have a degree in conservation rarely have any practical experience of breeding tropical butterflies. Secondly, the resources required to conserve butterflies may be substantial when concentrated in one place and rarely available in the natural tropical habitats of the butterflies.

The flowers of Pentas lanceolata graced by the tropical South American Siproeta stelenes.

Ecotourism, where a large amount of money is spent by tourists for a week or two's photographic holiday in a tropical environment, may assist the conservation of large animals, but it is a very inefficient way of spending resources to conserve butterflies. Attracting large numbers of people to any area usually results in habitat destruction and promotes the commercial development of nearby areas. Only a small proportion of the cost of such 'holidays' actually ends up in the hands of conservationists, and negligible amounts become available for butterfly conservation. In any case, there are very many people who, for reasons of health, disability, finance or personal commitments, are unable to visit tropical environments. A living tropical greenhouse enables everyone with a greenhouse or conservatory to be directly involved with tropical butterflies.

Most butterflies are inherently very suitable for conservation by breeding programmes in protected environments. An adult female will lay dozens, perhaps hundreds, of ova. Even under

A colony of common tropical American heliconid butterflies can be easily established even in a small greenhouse.

'natural' conditions in the wild, almost all of these will fail to reach the adult stage. If habitats and foodplants are destroyed, none of them will. Yet we know that human skills allow us to grow almost every species of plant, given the right conditions, even in countries far removed from the plants' country of origin.

These three species of tropical Asian swallowtails are currently common, but will they be so for long?

Papilio demoleus *(the chequered or lime swallowtail) is widespread in South-east Asia.*

A few successful butterfly farms have been set up in tropical countries, providing income for people living there and at the same time allowing large numbers of individuals of even rare species to be bred. But the number of species that can be saved in this way is small. This is largely a problem of knowledge, practical expertise and financial resources.

People living in the more affluent, developed countries can play a significant role in saving the world's butterflies. Most people, for whatever reason, will be unable actually to live and work in the areas of the world that are most at risk. To develop the practical expertise and knowledge required and to educate others about the true nature of tropical butterflies requires hands-on experience.

The purpose of this book is to show readers the possibilities and to point them in the right direction. Anyone who has established a living tropical greenhouse and actually bred tropical butterflies, having them living, breeding and free-flying in that protected environment, will gain more than mere knowledge. They will discover a great deal about themselves, and Gaia, with every flutter of the butterflies' wings. After that, we have faith in our readers to do what is right for plants, for the butterflies and even, perhaps, for humanity itself.

1 Setting up the greenhouse

The tailed jay needs plenty of sunlight to be active.

There tends to be a wide gulf between those who have a greenhouse and like to grow plants and those who are interested in invertebrates. There are many more gardeners than there are 'bug' breeders, and the former like to keep their greenhouses free from creatures that eat plants. Those with a genuine love of both butterflies and plants can bridge this gap.

The right system

Bug enthusiasts usually rear their livestock in small containers made from plastic or glass and keep them indoors in a suitable heated room. The situation for those who want to breed tropical butterflies is not so simple. It is true that if a supply of ova or larvae is available, it would be possible to take them through to the adult stage in quite small containers using potted plants or shoots cut from plants growing outside. To mate and lay ova, however, the adults need much more room. Many adult butterflies are not active unless the sun is out and often the pre-nuptial flight (perhaps 'chase' is a better word) requires a lot of space. In some countries, and at some times of the year, a large netted enclosure might be suitable, but in most temperate climates it is essential to have a heated greenhouse available if you wish to set up a long-term breeding colony. We do not consider other systems in this book.

The structure

It is possible to use any type of greenhouse. Anything less than about 1.80 x 1.80m (6 x 6ft) is likely to be too small, because the temperature will vary too rapidly, especially during sunny periods when excessive heat will build up in the greenhouse. It would, of course, be cheaper to maintain a desired minimum temperature in a small greenhouse.

If there is only space for a small greenhouse, an octagonal one will allow adult butterflies to fly round and round instead of coming to a halt at square corners. This shape is usually more expensive, so if the ground space is available a larger rectangular greenhouse would be more sensible. Whatever size you choose, it is almost inevitable that you will soon want a larger one.

The choice of material

Greenhouses can be made of many different materials. The choice of material will affect how much it will cost, how easy it is to adapt and how long it will last. Cheap greenhouses of thin galvanized steel soon begin to rust because the atmosphere in a tropical greenhouse is likely to be very humid. Small greenhouses with light frames and covered with clear plastic will rarely last more than a year or two, depending on the outside climate and conditions. Even the 'UV-stabilized' plastics will deteriorate, especially with increasing UV radiation due to depletion of the ozone layer. Good plants can be grown in plastic-covered tunnel greenhouses, but these do not look very nice in an ordinary garden; the plastic does not

last indefinitely and it can be difficult to keep the conditions inside suitable for all stages of a butterfly's life-cycle.

A greenhouse made of aluminium is easy to erect and all manner of shapes and sizes are available. Models are always changing, as well as the names of the manufacturers. Most are sold as complete entities rather than as units that can be put together to make up a larger one. It may be

This magnificent tropical greenhouse at Staunton Country Park, Hampshire, England, was reconstructed in Victorian style at great expense.

You can establish a living tropical greenhouse in a very small structure.

possible to join together models from two separate manufacturers, but this is not easy. Size is important and the largest is often the best buy. There never seems to be enough space for everything you want. Ordinary horticultural glass is the cheapest. Safety glass may be more appropriate to your needs and conditions, but it will be much dearer. Double- or triple-wall plastic sheeting is available for a few greenhouses, but is also expensive and cannot be fitted into every type of frame. Some of the larger sizes of greenhouse may be available with this option, but smaller sizes may not.

Inside a cedarwood living tropical greenhouse.

Wood has better insulation properties than metal and it is easier to attach things to it. Ordinary wood does not last very long under warm and humid conditions even when it has been treated with preservatives. (Remember that toxic chemicals should not be used once the structure is set up as a living tropical greenhouse.) The best material is cedarwood, because it contains its own natural preservatives. The glazing bars of wooden greenhouses are thicker than those of aluminium ones and this cuts down the light a little. In general, a cedarwood greenhouse is more attractive to look at from the outside, especially in a small garden. Unfortunately, cedarwood is not very strong and it is only suitable for squat greenhouses which are not very wide. They can, however, be as long as you want.

A brick foundation is good for any greenhouse, but a wall can only be used to increase the height of specially designed greenhouses unless you want to have steps for going in and out, and these take up valuable space.

The sides

Whatever type of greenhouse you choose, it is better to have vertical sides than sloping ('Dutch light') ones. Although the sloping sides allow more light into the greenhouse, they reduce the space available at the top for the butterflies to fly in and they also make the necessary climbing plants overhang the space that you will be walking in. Sloping sides also encourage the butterflies to fly down to the bottom, as they do in plastic tunnels. The air down there will usually be colder and damper and the butterflies may have difficulty getting active again. They will also be vulnerable to ground-dwelling predators. These disadvantages probably outweigh the rather small gain in light. Whatever the type of greenhouse, it is necessary to have as many opening windows (vents) as possible.

Conservatories

Conservatories are generally made to much higher standards than greenhouses. They are usually intended for use as extended living areas rather than for the growth of plants alone. This does not prohibit their use as living tropical greenhouses and the remarks already made in the above paragraphs are equally valid. Conservatories are usually placed against an existing wall, but there is no reason why a free-standing structure of the same quality cannot be obtained if sufficient funds are available. Those fitted with sealed-unit double glazing will obviously have a superior ability to retain heat during the colder months. Problems may arise during hot, sunny weather because they may have inadequate facilities for ventilation. It can be difficult to fit secondary netted doors which will allow you to leave the original door open. It would be wise to choose a structure of aluminium, with proper 'heat-breaks' between the inside and outside as well as double glazing. Hardwood conservatories may suffer in the warm, humid conditions of a living tropical greenhouse. Many conservatories are fitted with internal blinds; these are not suitable because butterflies can become trapped between them and the glass.

With modern lighting systems, which can replace natural sunlight if necessary, it is also possible to establish a living tropical greenhouse system in a structure with very little natural illumination. The Victorians were fond of elegant structures called orangeries and it is sad to note that almost all of those that have survived to the present time have been turned into exhibition halls, cafés or craft areas rather than being used for their original purpose. They would make ideal living tropical greenhouses.

Siting the structure

Identifying the best site for a living tropical greenhouse is not easy. A small garden may have only one place in it that is suitable. Shading by trees, walls or houses may be a problem, but a very exposed site could lead to wind damage or rapid heat loss. Beware of putting a greenhouse near to a boundary fence. The people next door may plant a tree or a hedge at the edge of their property and not keep it cut to a reasonable height. You may like the look of your greenhouse, but others may not. Unless you are investing heavily in electrical lighting units, natural sunlight is necessary, but it need not be over the whole of

The glasswing butterfly, Greta oto, *prefers a greenhouse that is not fully exposed to direct sunlight.*

the greenhouse for all the hours of daylight.

Early morning and evening sun supplies much-needed heat, but mid-day sun can provide too much and you will need external blinds for shading or lots of ventilation. For this reason, the classic east-west orientation may not be ideal in summer although it is desirable in winter. You need to consider seriously the daily and seasonal movement of the direction from which the sunlight comes and memory alone is rarely sufficient.

You should also choose a location that allows access to an electricity supply and piped water.

Although rain water is much to be preferred, it is unlikely that the supply from the greenhouse roof will be sufficient in the summer.

If at all possible, have the door away from the sun; this will help prevent butterflies congregating near the door, which can result in accidental escapes.

Relocating the greenhouse

In many cases, it may be that the greenhouse is already in place. Taking apart a nailed wooden greenhouse is likely to damage the structure and even screws may be rusted and difficult to remove. Glass that has been held in with putty is also likely to be stubborn. An aluminium greenhouse

A second, netted door allows the main door to be left open for ventilation.

that is bolted together is easier to deal with. The clips holding the glass can usually be removed easily, especially if they are of the spring-wire type. The frame may then be light enough for two or three people to move. You can slide long fencing posts under it and move the whole thing to a better place, if this is desirable.

Fixing it to the ground

A greenhouse presents a large surface area to the wind and it is sensible to follow carefully the manufacturer's instructions regarding the way in which the structure is held to the ground. It is always desirable to have a good brick base even when a 'base' is supplied with the greenhouse. We prefer to attach any metal base with a number of bolts that have been cemented into the brick foundations. Should the need arise to move the greenhouse, these can then be undone. It is easier than having to dig out spikes embedded in solid concrete. Whether the greenhouse is located on a concrete slab or on to bare soil is a point of debate. A slab allows the inside of the greenhouse to be cleaned thoroughly and may reduce pest problems, but the plants will have to be in containers and will need more care and attention. Some plants do seem to like a free run for their roots.

Netting and ventilation

Any windows that can be opened must be fitted with very fine netting. The law does not allow the intentional liberation of species that do not occur naturally in a country. In addition it is essential to prevent the entry of native creatures, many of them very tiny insects, that would attack and kill various stages of a butterfly's life-cycle or the plants themselves. You will need netting that is fine

Papilio aegeus *(the orchard swallowtail) brightens up any greenhouse.*

enough to stop whitefly getting in. The way the netting is attached depends on the material the greenhouse is made of. Non-ferrous metal and plastic are good materials, but wood will require treatment to prevent it rotting in the humid atmosphere. It is not sufficient merely to stretch netting across the opening, because the windows have to be opened and closed. You can purchase units that will open ventilation windows automatically, but they must be taken into account when you net the windows. Always check the range of temperatures over which they open to make sure it is high enough for your tropical conditions. Most netting will deteriorate in sunlight and automatic vent openers do go wrong from time to time, so expect to have to change them in the future. Fit them to the sunny side of the greenhouse or they will be slow to open. Adjustment is usually on a trial-and-error basis. Although more expensive, initially, it is well worth installing a thermostatically controlled fan for

ventilation. Apart from its use in cooling, regular changes of air do make for healthier plants.

Doors

Getting into the greenhouse means opening the doors, even if they are not also an essential part of the ventilation system. Simple curtains of net help, but will not stay in place. A plastic strip or bead curtain may help, but will not be sufficient on its own, even with heavy-duty plastic strips. It is best to fit an additional door consisting of a light-weight frame with 5 or 10mm ($^1/4$ or $^1/2$in) metal mesh covered with fine netting. Without the metal mesh, large animals may break into your greenhouse when you are elsewhere. If an additional door is not possible, try putting a wooden frame around the door and attach some suitable material to it. You can use a zip or some other method to open and close it. If space is available, an outer netted vestibule with its own door is an ideal solution to problems of access.

2   Heating and growth media

In general it is easier to create conditions for good plant growth than for prolific butterfly breeding.

What do butterflies need?

Nobody agrees on what exactly constitutes the optimum conditions for a tropical greenhouse. It is not synonymous with 'tropical rainforest'. Weather conditions differ widely in the various regions of the tropics. Most climatic data that is readily available refers to large cities or averages for very large areas. Only a few butterflies complete their life-cycle in large cities and it is likely that they are tolerating such conditions rather than becoming adapted to them. In any case an average temperature or rainfall does not describe the variations that occur across the 24 hours of the day and night, nor between one site and another in a region.

Even when a particular natural habitat has been described from a vegetational aspect, it is not likely that a detailed record is available of the precise conditions that all stages of the butterfly life-cycle prefer. It would be hard to define the best conditions even for butterflies from temperate climates. The natural changes of the seasons have been a significant influence in the evolution of butterfly life-cycles. In the living tropical greenhouse, unless we have unlimited financial resources, we can only hope to provide a tolerable microclimate for our plants and butterflies. In this book we take a very broad view of what constitutes both a tropical butterfly and a tropical climate.

Many aspects must be considered when creating a satisfactory environment for both plants and butterflies. What are the minimum, maximum and optimum temperatures? How much light do they need and for how long? What type of soil and water do the plants need and what plants do the butterflies require? How do all these factors interact?

Heating

Fortunately, there is not just one optimal temperature for all tropical butterflies. This is probably just as well, because if there was such a temperature it would be almost impossible to keep it constant all day and night. Heat reaches the greenhouse from the sun and this can be supplemented with heaters inside. Because the outside is usually colder than the inside, heat will leak out of the greenhouse, the amount depending on its construction, materials and other factors.

The temperature outside a greenhouse is rarely constant and will change with time of day and season, often in a very unpredictable way due to a host of factors. In general, we need to provide a temperature between 25 and 30°C (77 and 86°F) if our tropical butterflies are to fly actively. In sunlight this is easy, but could be rapidly exceeded. Actually, the vast majority of plants are not as efficient at photosynthesis above 25°C (77°F). Above 30°C (86°F) you will have to switch on cooling fans and open windows or doors. Because this will also result in a reduction in the humidity inside the greenhouse, it is better if the sun's rays can be limited at peak times by external roller blinds. For most small greenhouses these will be manually operated, but automatic ones are available. You can paint traditional white greenhouse shading on to the glass when prolonged periods of bright sunlight are expected. Small greenhouses will inevitably experience greater fluctuations of temperature than large ones, although it should be remembered that the heat capacity of air is very low, so it does not take much heat to raise air temperature compared to soil and water.

It makes sense to make the most efficient use of the sun's heat. Some people even suggest putting large containers of water in the greenhouse to store the heat, which will then be slowly liberated during the night. However, few greenhouses are large enough for this. The Victorians often had large water reservoirs under the floor, serving as both humidifiers and heat stores. Solar heating panels might also be useful if the greenhouse structure is suitable and the visible light not drastically reduced by them. Pots, soil, and brick or concrete bases will also store heat. It is generally considered that a heater with a capacity equivalent to about 3 kilowatts is

External roller blinds, automatic vents and bubble plastic insulation all help to control the temperature.

required in a 3.8 x 3.0m (about 12 x 10ft) insulated greenhouse, in a moderately temperate climate. This will maintain the sort of temperatures required during winter months.

Thermostatic control is necessary and the limits to the power that can be taken from a mains electrical supply should be considered. It must be remembered that electricity and water are a dangerous combination and any electrical work and equipment must be installed to the highest safety standards.

Distribution of the heat generally requires fans or a fan heater, to avoid local overheating. In a still atmosphere, heat will rise and the ground and low plants will stay cold. The Victorians often used external solid-fuel boilers with large water pipes to carry the heat around their greenhouses. Very hot pipes are not desirable, but modern systems with underground plastic pipes could be considered if finances allow for such an installation. The required heat input needs to be calculated carefully, as with all heating systems. Piped systems do not dry the air in the way that simple fan heaters do.

The relative costs, benefits and disadvantages of various fuels and heating systems are largely influenced by local factors. Electric heaters do not give out water or fumes, but liquid and solid fuels do. Combustion requires air, and it is essential that there is an adequate air supply to any form of flame otherwise the fuel may burn incompletely and carbon monoxide gas will be produced. This is very dangerous, because it is poisonous but cannot be seen and has no odour. Some heat will be lost from the inlet vent, but inlets are essential. When used to maintain the high temperatures needed in a living tropical greenhouse, any burning of fuel will produce quite a lot of water (how much can be calculated) as well as carbon dioxide, although the latter may be beneficial for plant growth. It is essential that complete combustion is obtained with any fuel to avoid the dangers of carbon monoxide poisoning. Proper safety advice by a qualified person is essential for any fuel burning appliance and the temperatures that are required must be taken into account when you are considering burner capacity. Obviously, an external combustion system with hot air or water ducted to the inside of the greenhouse would overcome some of these problems.

Insulation

If the inside of the greenhouse is going to be kept at a higher temperature than the outside, then insulation will be needed if the heating costs are to be kept to reasonable limits. Built-in features, such as double glazing with sealed glass units and heat-loss barriers on the framework, as used in some conservatories, would be ideal, but, apart from the expense, cannot be fitted to most greenhouses. Probably the cheapest insulation material is that packing material which consists of air trapped in bubbles between plastic sheets. This may last for a few years if it has been treated with stabilizers that prevent the harmful effects of ultraviolet light. It will reduce heat loss by about

Except for the door, the outside of this octagonal greenhouse has been covered with plastic bubble wrap. Putting it on the inside creates gaps in which butterflies can become trapped.

50%, but also reduces the amount of light reaching the plants. Single sheets of clear plastic materials can also be used, but will be less effective.

Virtually all these materials become brittle with age and need replacing from time to time. There must be no gaps or slits in the insulation through which the butterflies can creep, because they will get stuck between the glass and the sheeting. On the shady side of a greenhouse it may be worth using a reflective material with an insulated backing, as used in artificially lit plant growth rooms. A cheaper alternative is shiny kitchen foil on top of bubble wrap insulation. If this is used on the side of the greenhouse where the sun does not shine, it may help to reflect heat and light back into the interior.

Heating cables

Obviously heating costs will vary depending on the size of the greenhouse, its location, the outside temperature and other climatic factors. The operation of any living tropical greenhouse is subject to financial constraints. Heating the air is much easier than heating the ground and electrical heating cables should be considered because soil temperature has a large effect on root function and plant growth. Obviously, you must take care not to damage underground heating cables while digging. Ordinary domestic soil heating cable provides very little heat per unit length and a very long length would be required to significantly influence the temperature of the whole greenhouse.

Night-time temperatures

It is not at all easy to decide on the lowest temperature that a butterfly greenhouse can be allowed to reach. In the outside environment it is almost always cooler at night. This is good for the plants because it allows them to make up any water shortage that has arisen during a hot day, and it also reduces the rate of plant respiration.

A rather similar daily cycle of the temperature is likely to take place in a heated greenhouse. Most heaters do not have an easy method for setting different temperatures for the day and night. This is a job that usually has to be done

Larvae of the giant owl butterflies need high night-time temperatures for feeding.

manually. If the heaters have sufficient capacity, it is possible to keep the same temperature both night and day. A few larvae, such as those of *Caligo* species, feed almost entirely at night and need a high temperature then.

It might be thought that tender plants of the type that we have in a butterfly greenhouse would merely need to be protected from frost and so a temperature just above 0°C (32°F) would be adequate. This is not the case, because many tropical plants are damaged at temperatures well above freezing, especially if the soil is damp and conditions are humid. We would recommend a temperature of 13°C (55.4°F) if you have *Musa velutina* and some of the more tender species of *Passiflora*. If you are growing passion flowers, you should consult a good book on the subject. Nursery catalogues are also useful.

At the temperature suggested above, none of the stages of the life-cycle of tropical butterflies will normally be active, but most will tolerate it overnight and solar gain will generally increase the temperature during the daylight hours. If you know that the temperature in the greenhouse is going to drop, it is best to cut back most soft, leafy growth to help prevent serious mould growth on damaged leaves. Dormant buds and

A maximum and minimum thermometer is essential, but it needs to be carefully placed out of direct sunlight.

roots are generally better able to withstand low temperatures and will probably grow out again under warmer conditions. Always try to match plants to the conditions. Know your plants!

Musa uranoscopus, *a small border banana species, needs high temperatures.*

Soil or not

Although some butterflies like to perch on the surface of muddy soil and may even take essential minerals from it, the presence of soil is not essential in a living tropical greenhouse.

Soil-less systems

It is possible to grow plants without any soil using a number of hydroculture systems. Commercial growers of, for example, greenhouse tomatoes frequently use such soil-less systems and often produce excellent plants. Such systems require study and careful consideration before they are installed and there is not space in this book to discuss them in detail. Some systems use pots or troughs, without holes in the bottom, and an inert support for the roots, such as expanded clay. A small quantity of a complete liquid feed is kept at the bottom of the container and has to be replaced when it is used up, which means that it must be checked frequently. Some have special containers with floats or dipsticks to make this easier. A similar system has an external reservoir from which the liquid feed is periodically pumped into the plant container and then drained away. A third system, called Nutrient Film Technique (NFT for short) has a slightly sloping trough along which a thin film of the liquid feed is continuously flowing, fed from a pump in an external reservoir. The plants are started off in small cubes of an inert porous material, such as the mineral known as rock wool, but the roots will grow into dense mats in the troughs.

Solid floor alternatives

If your greenhouse has a solid floor, of slabs or concrete, a hydroponic system is worth considering. Otherwise, you should go over to plants in conventional pots. Another alternative is raised beds, whether the base beneath is soil or not.

Your soil

Ordinary garden soil varies enormously from place to place and the gardener must take account of this. It may harbour various plant pests and diseases as well as predators that might kill the butterflies at various stages of their life-cycle. It is difficult to get rid of these things with non-persistent pesticide chemicals and you should consult a local garden supplies centre if you decide to do so. Take care not to use any long-lasting toxic products, nor any that might be taken up by the plants. Remember that a butterfly greenhouse will be run along the non-pesticide principles of organic gardening and it would be as well to start off that way.

Before you do anything, however, you should find out what type of soil you have in the greenhouse. The suitability of the soil will depend, in the first instance, on the size and relative proportions of the mineral particles that make up the soil – what is called the mechanical analysis of the soil. In the wild, most *Passiflora* species grow in well-drained, sandy soil often not particularly rich in plant nutrients. This means that if your soil has a large proportion of clay in it, passion flowers will not like it. Many plants you grow will be under stress because the larvae will be eating the leaves, so plants do need to develop good root systems. If the original soil is not suitable you can try to improve it or replace it entirely. A depth of soil of between 30 and 60cm (12 and 24in) will be adequate for most domestic greenhouses. To improve what you have already, some of it will have to be removed and replaced with something appropriate. Coarse and potting grit will improve drainage and a soil-less compost, peat or peat substitute, will add organic matter that will help to hold moisture. Obviously local conditions will dictate what you actually do. Remember that inorganic grit will last for ever, but organic materials will soon disappear in a tropical greenhouse. There are many alternatives for improving soil texture and water-holding capacity and for allowing the essential creation of air spaces in the soil.

Getting the soil right before you even start is important. Once the plants are in, it is very difficult to change the soil. Any soil with clay in it is likely to get waterlogged and compacted, and if you have that type of soil you will need to get rid of it entirely. Take a small lump of your soil and wet it. If it sticks together and feels slippery it will have clay in it. When you have taken out any soil you do not want, give some attention to drainage at the bottom before you replace it with new soil, otherwise you may be creating an underground pond when you water the plants. We recommend that you make up your own soil mixture from basic constituents bought separately: sterile good-quality potting soil, sterile peat or peat substitutes and various grades of potting and horticultural grit. Take care when incorporating 'organic' materials and manures that they are sterile, because you may be adding pests, diseases or

This Junonia octavia *from South Africa is seeking minerals from a patch of bare, damp soil.*

other problems along with them. In general, we do not recommend that you buy a large batch of what is popularly described as 'top soil' because there is no precise definition of what this is. It may prove to be quite unsuitable for a living tropical greenhouse.

Plants in pots

Plants that are in pots can be moved to better locations in the greenhouse or rested outside. Pots vary a great deal in size and shape and it is up to you what you use, but remember that spiders can hide under the rims and slugs and other creatures under the bases. Our previous remarks on soil also apply to potting composts and it is desirable to incorporate a coated fertilizer for release over a long period of time. The type of compost can vary from one pot to another to suit the plants. Some may prefer a lime-free compost. Soil-less composts are easier to re-wet if they contain water-holding gels. Watering from the base rather than the top also helps. Some plants benefit from having a tray under the pot, but others do not, and this is largely a matter of the interaction between the plant, the soil and the way you maintain your greenhouse environment.

3 Light and water

The hop tree, Ptelea trifoliata, *of the citrus family, has strongly scented flowers but loses its leaves in winter.*

Glass lets light in to a greenhouse and it is tempting to think that we need not give it any further consideration. This is very far from the truth, because what we casually refer to as light is actually very complicated and affects butterflies and plants in different ways. Much more is known about the way light affects plants than about how it affects butterflies. Very little of the published research on plants has, however, been carried out on plants that are of interest to the creator of a living tropical greenhouse and so we have to extrapolate from the known to the unknown, using general principles. The same is true for butterflies, where much of the work has been carried out on a few species that are pests of commercial crops. How the effect of light on the plants can indirectly affect the butterflies has hardly been researched at all. The situation is even more complex, for both plants and butterflies, because there may be additional interactions between temperature and light.

Light periods

When plants that are not native to the tropics are grown in a heated greenhouse, some will still lose their leaves in what is the autumn period, even when the temperature inside the greenhouse has been kept at tropical values. This is due to the time for which the light is available, also known as the duration of the light period. In some species, the time at which plants flower is also influenced by the duration of the light period.

Long and short days

Although in the tropics the duration of the sunlight hours does not vary very much, the further a place is from the equator the greater the difference between summer and winter due to the way that the Earth rotates with respect to the sun. Near the equator there are roughly 12 hours of light and 12 of darkness in each day. Moving away from the equator in either direction results in summer daylight hours that are longer (called long days by botanists, although a day is still 24 hours in total) and winter daylight hours that are shorter (short days). This is the same from one year to the next with predictable changes from day to day and it has been selected by evolution as a cue for changes in the life-cycle of many plants and animals. This is because the return of colder and less favourable conditions in temperate climates is always preceded by shortening daylength.

Butterflies and plants from the tropics will not have evolved under these conditions and will not use daylength as a signal to influence their life-cycle, although they may use other signals, such as water supply or temperature. This means that if

It is not known whether these larvae of Papilio polytes *feeding on citrus can sense daylength directly or through the plant leaves.*

we keep conditions in the living tropical greenhouse constant, we can have a continuous succession of broods all year round, as happens naturally with some species in the tropics. For the butterflies, this probably means never letting the number of hours of light fall below 12, which can only be done in temperate regions by using artificial lighting. It is not known for certain whether all butterflies measure the length of time that the light is on, but we do know that plants have a mechanism for measuring how long the light is off. This is in the leaves, and the plant responds to shortening days long before the leaves fall off. Butterfly larvae feeding on the leaves may detect these changes in their foodplant long before we can detect them.

Although artificial lighting can be switched on or off in a fraction of a second, this does not happen with sunlight; it changes gradually during dawn and dusk. Giant owl butterflies (species in the genus *Caligo*) tend to fly at these times rather than in full sun. Other adult butterflies may also have a preferred time for flying, mating or laying ova which may be related to the amount of light or the temperature.

Kalanchoe blossfeldiana *is a useful plant in a living tropical greenhouse, because it flowers in short days.*

Cold periods

Obviously, if a temperate zone plant has lost its leaves during the autumn, it cannot use them to detect the end of winter by the lengthening days of spring. In any case this would be a hazardous method, because the weather conditions in spring are not always suitable for growth. Evolution has selected a method based on the length of time for which it has been cold, and the dormant plant will not start into growth again unless it has been exposed to a suitable period of low temperatures. This has normally taken place before it gets warm, so the plant is ready to grow as soon as temperatures rise.

A dormant plant that has not had the cold period that it needs may be very reluctant to start growing again. Diapausing butterfly pupae may also only come to life again after a cool period of rest. What exactly constitutes a cold (or cool) period is not clearly defined, but in general a temperature between 5 and 10°C (41 and 50°F) for several weeks is sufficient for most temperate zone plants.

The black wings on this Papilio polytes *help it to warm up more quickly in sunlight.*

Losing leaves

As you would expect, many of the plants in a tropical greenhouse are not very sensitive to daylength changes. They may lose their leaves due to stress from drought, too much water, shortage of nutrients, damage, or low light intensities. In these cases it is usually the older leaves that are lost. So-called 'evergreen' plants do lose their older leaves, but not in one go and not necessarily every year. Old leaves often accumulate high levels of toxic biochemicals and become unpalatable to larvae, although in some plants it is the young leaves that may be less palatable.

A plant grows by producing sugars from carbon dioxide and water with energy derived from light. The amount of light (its intensity) is one significant factor, but other factors, such as the temperature and the humidity, are also important. Under any given set of conditions, only one of the factors will be limiting, and increasing the other factors will not result in better growth. Heating the greenhouse to high temperatures in the winter will not be beneficial unless there is so much light that it is temperature that is the limiting factor and not light. Apart from creating food reserves for growth when there is enough light, plants also use up their reserves by respiration, both day and night. The higher the temperature, the faster the respiration will use up the reserves.

In addition to all this, there is a process called photorespiration which wastes a plant's energy in the light when the temperature gets above about 25°C (77°F). Most plants are like this and only a few, not necessarily tropical ones, have evolved a mechanism to get round the problem. The answer is to provide as much light as possible in the winter and keep the temperature as low as possible, subject to the minimum demanded by the plants and, more so, by the butterflies. Butterflies use the energy in light to supplement heat generated by flapping the wings and so get airborne. The black markings on the wings of some of the tropical swallowtails is one way to ensure that the maximum amount of heating is obtained from light. An insulation to keep the heat in is likely to reduce the amount of light available by a significant amount. Using a light meter inside and outside will give some idea of the reduction you are getting, but to measure the amount of light available for photosynthesis requires a special type of light meter called a PAR (Photosynthetically Active Radiation) meter.

Wavelengths

This brings us to another aspect of light that we must consider, especially if we are going to use electric lights to overcome a shortage of natural light in winter. Photographers will be familiar with the fact that you cannot take good pictures indoors using ordinary tungsten filament bulbs to replace sunlight unless you use special filters or film. This is sometimes described as relating to the 'colour temperature' of the light source, but is more clearly understood as relating to the wavelengths that make up the light.

Sunlight has a very wide distribution of wavelengths, those in the region visible to humans being the colours of the rainbow, with a lot of energy also in the invisible ultraviolet and infrared regions. Botanists call this distribution of the energy in the light its 'quality'. The PAR meter measures those wavelengths that are important in photosynthesis, but not the energy in the ultraviolet and infrared. Plants can 'see' some of the infrared wavelengths and use their intensity in relation to other wavelengths for various purposes, such as directing their growth patterns towards what is appropriate in the natural world. Some tropical plants live in the shade and so do not alter their growth form when grown in reduced light, but others grow in the open and will become very tall and thin if grown under too little light or light of the wrong quality. When you use supplementary electric lighting, you must take into account not only the length of time it is on

Protective wire netting is needed to keep butterflies away from this 400-watt halide lamp which gives light of good quality and quantity but gets very hot.

for, but also the quantity and especially the quality of the light source. Ordinary domestic tungsten light bulbs are not suitable and the fittings will not be safe in a humid greenhouse.

Choosing a system

If you are going to buy electrical lighting systems to supplement natural daylight, you should learn something about them before spending money. Many aspects need to be considered apart from the type and size of the lamp and its holder, which must be of the drip-proof type. Get as much information as you can about the system you are thinking of purchasing. Much of the electrical power used by lights and their control gear ends up as heat and will contribute to the heating of a greenhouse. Some types of lamp are more efficient than others; that is, they give out more light per unit of electricity used. The table in this section gives some basic information about the commonly available types of lighting equipment. It is wise to consult a reputable specialist supplier before purchasing such equipment. It is rarely available from ordinary retailers.

Supplementary lighting for greenhouses: a few common types

Consult a supplier for costs and specific product details because there are many variations.

	Fluorescent Tubes	High Intensity Discharge Lamps			
		Mercury Tungsten Fluorescent	Mercury Fluorescent	Metal Halide	Sodium
Usual codes[1]	F	MTF	MF	MH	SON
Control gear[2]	Separate	Inside bulb	Separate	Separate	Separate
Typical wattages	18–40+ depending on length	100, 160	125, 400	400, 1,000	400, 1,000
Efficiency of light output in Lumens per watt[3]	Used in multiples to increase Lumens per unit area	10, 16 for above wattages	46, 50 for above wattages	71, 92 for above wattages	116, 123 for above wattages
Light quality variations[4]	Many types, e.g. white, warm white, Grolux	One type	One type	One type	Several types e.g. Agro, Plus, Planta

NOTES

1. Different manufacturers and suppliers have their own particular coding systems.

2. Control gear is generally specific to a particular type and wattage. Take expert advice on how many lights can be switched on at one time from your electrical supply because of large power surges when the lights start up.

3. For a single type of bulb, the higher the wattage, the more light that is produced, but the more expensive it is to run. Note that many different scientific units are used to measure light.

4. Many different types of reflector are available, but all fittings should be drip-proof. Light intensity falls off rapidly with distance from the bulb and slowly with the age of the bulb. Automatic tracks are available to move the lamps over the plants to get even illumination.

Ultraviolet light

Although ultraviolet light is likely to stunt plant growth if it is excessive and is not known to have much, if any, favourable effect on plants, it can be important for the butterflies. Their eyes are sensitive to it and they use it to see feeding guides in flowers. Many species also have ultraviolet-reflective scale patterns on their wings which may be important for recognizing individuals of the same species and sometimes their sex. Although it is possible to buy lights that give out a lot of ultraviolet light, these would not be suitable for the greenhouse because of the danger to human eyes and skin. If you decide to use mercury vapour lamps, always ensure that the bulb has a fluorescent coating on it that will convert the ultraviolet light produced into visible light before it gets out of the bulb. With some natural sunlight entering the greenhouse it is likely that the butterflies will have enough to see with.

Water

Plants and butterflies need water to survive and grow. Water can exist in three forms: solid, liquid and vapour, although the first is not of interest in the living tropical greenhouse. Liquid water is a very good solvent and will dissolve all sorts of substances that it comes into contact with on its way to the greenhouse. Hence there are many variations to be found in liquid water.

Water vapour, on the other hand, is pure water and if it is condensed under very clean conditions it is called distilled water. This is not very good for plants, because it contains no plant nutrients and if used excessively would leach the nutrients out of the compost and away from the plant roots. It is good, however, for making up fertilizer solutions, because it does not contain substances, such as calcium, that might precipitate out plant nutrients from solution. The next best thing is clean rain water which, although it comes from water vapour, will have dissolved substances present in the air and in the water barrel before you come to use it. Keep the barrel as clean as you can and always covered to keep things from falling into it. If rain water is collected near trees it will contain some plant nutrients leached out of

Large tropical greenhouses can have large water features.

the leaves, if near the sea it will have some salt in it and if near a source of pollution it will contain the pollutants, such as the various oxides that might make it into acid rain. If you are using reasonable amounts of fertilizer, this will probably not be a problem unless the water is very acidic.

When it comes to tap water, soft water is better than hard, but you will have little choice

Small waterfalls or fountains are a good way of increasing humidity, if there is sufficient room.

botanist. The main problem with hard water is that the calcium salts it contains may build up in the pot, even forming a crust on the surface of the soil, and it may also produce nutrient deficiency symptoms in plants. Let tap water stand for as long as possible before you use it to let the chlorine dissipate, and if it is of the hard type hang a netting bag full of peat in the tank to help counteract the excessive calcium. Try to use water that has been warmed to the same temperature as the greenhouse soil, perhaps by storing a few days' supply in the greenhouse itself. It is not good to pour cold water on to the leaves or even the soil of a wilting plant.

Water vapour

The amount of water vapour in the air is expressed by the term 'percentage relative humidity' (RH%). As the temperature of the air increases, it can hold more water vapour, so there is more water in a given volume of air at 30°C (86°F) than at 20°C (68°F) when both are at 100 RH%. If the temperature is not exactly the same all over the greenhouse, which it never is, the additional water will condense out as a liquid. This makes some places very wet; butterfly larvae may drown and adults may get stuck to the glass by their wings and die. It is not good to have too high a relative humidity, but neither is it good for it to be too low, because plants, but more especially the butterflies at all stages of their life-cycle, will dry up and die. Obviously the RH% will vary with the time of day, as the temperature does. You should keep a good hygrometer in the greenhouse and attempt to keep the humidity in the range from, say, 60 to 90 RH% at all times, but remember that it will never be constant for long.

over what is in your local tap water. Certainly substances are added to it to make it safe to drink, on top of what was in it before it was treated. You can obtain a detailed analysis from your water supplier, but it may not make much sense to you unless you are both a chemist and a

Controlling humidity

Keeping the humidity down is not a problem unless the rain is getting in and saturating everything. Opening windows or doors will usually lower humidity should that prove necessary and if it is compatible with the temperature requirements. Water features such as small fountains will help to raise humidity and provide a place where adult butterflies can drink, which they need to do from time to time. Gravel or paved paths can be watered with a can to raise humidity, but it is not advisable to wet the soil itself too much as this may adversely affect plant growth. Installing an overhead mist spray system is an ideal solution, but requires some thought. Fully plumbed mains-operated systems with a humidity sensor control to prevent over-watering are an ideal solution, but expensive. A cheap, hand-controlled system using plastic piping may prove satisfactory if someone is on hand to work it. It is necessary to have a very good connecting arrangement for individual sections, otherwise joints may blow open due to changes in water pressure, especially on hot days when the plastic tubing can become rather too flexible.

A spray system must produce very fine droplets of water otherwise butterflies will be injured. If there are several sections, it may help to have them with individual in-line taps so that some can be shut off if desirable, for example, to prevent getting too much water on a plant that has young larvae on it. If rain water is used, then a suitable pump will be necessary to develop sufficient pressure as well as an in-line filter to catch any particles. If there is not someone always available to water the plants, you may need an appropriate automatic or semi-automatic system.

There are many such systems available, differing widely in design and price. In hard-water areas the fine jets may clog up, so you should be able to remove them for cleaning. Using a mist system will rapidly cool the air in a greenhouse, so short bursts are better than a long spray. Butterflies will fly in the spray, provided it is fine enough and does not go on for very long. Getting a very fine spray requires a high water pressure.

A fine mist spray is the best way to increase humidity.

4 Planting up the greenhouse

The plant in its place

Plants need to get well established before they become food for larvae or before they will flower profusely. It is important to get them in as soon as possible, but it is also essential to put them in the right place. In general, nectar plants need to have plenty of light, while some larval foodplants need to be in less sunny positions, both for the benefit of the plants and the larvae that will eat them. Obviously, tall, large-leaved plants will block out the light for anything in their shade. Plants that are not eaten may grow very large in a tropical greenhouse and may require pruning.

Unless you have obtained plants from an

The Egyptian star cluster, Pentas lanceolata, *is an excellent plant for nectar; it flowers almost all year round.*

organic grower who does not use pesticides, it will be necessary to let the plants grow for about six months before they are eaten. Almost all commercial nursery plants and imported plants will have been treated with systemic insecticides. These get inside the plant and are transported to growing parts and cannot simply be washed off the outside. Commercial growers have suffered great losses due to the activity of the vine weevil, whose grubs live in the soil and destroy the roots, so most plants sold in pots will be in a compost that contains added insecticides. It is prudent to replace this with fresh potting compost. Read the labels carefully on anything you buy. Do not, of course, use the pest-control 'sticks' that can be pushed into the soil where they liberate a systemic insecticide that is taken up by the plant's roots. This doesn't mean that it is good to bring into the greenhouse plants that have pests on them. Thrips, for example, are difficult to see, but can rapidly increase to plague proportions.

Stachytarpheta mutabilis *can be grown easily from seed and is a good nectar plant for butterflies.*

Getting started

There are three ways to get started with the plants: by seed, by cuttings and by obtaining plants that are already well grown. Seed is usually the cheapest and most readily available source of unusual plants. The main problems relate to the gradual loss of viability that always occurs during storage. In general, the cooler and drier the conditions in which the seeds are stored, the longer they will retain their ability to germinate. However, some tropical plants have seeds that cannot be allowed to dry too much and which will only keep for a few months under any conditions.

If possible, obtain the seed from someone who is actually growing the plant and can be sure that it is reasonably fresh and has been kept under good conditions. The seeds of unusual plants are not generally covered by regulations that stipulate what percentage of germination there must be or the date by which they should be sown. The situation is further complicated by the fact that some seeds have an inbuilt dormancy which does not allow them to germinate until certain precise conditions have been met. Thus it is almost impossible to decide whether an unusual seed is just dormant or dead.

The commonly cultivated garden flowers and vegetables are selected so that their seeds germinate quickly under most conditions and without a dormancy period.

Cuttings

Some plants can be easily propagated from cuttings under the simplest of conditions and others may require considerable skill and special conditions. Starting from cuttings is only recommended if you already have an established plant as a source of cuttings or can obtain them from someone who has. It is beyond the scope of this small book to give a detailed account of the propagation of even the few plants mentioned in it, let alone the virtually unlimited range of species that you might want to grow in your living tropical greenhouse.

In the pot

It is easier to start with pot- (or container-) grown plants that are of a reasonable size. If you start them off many months before you introduce any butterflies into the greenhouse, it is likely that any pesticides in or on them will have dissipated, especially if you have carried out some pruning of the older parts to encourage new growth. It is worth remembering what was said earlier in the book, that many deciduous-leaved plants may keep their leaves longer than usual in a heated greenhouse, and overwintering dormant buds may not open next spring because they have not had their winter 'cold treatment'. Others may be forced into premature early growth, which can seriously weaken the plants, especially if the leaves are eaten.

Plants for nectar

The plants that can be grown in a living tropical greenhouse can be placed into various categories. Some will provide nectar from their flowers that most, but not all, butterflies will need. You will require a constant supply of nectar and this may be obtained by having some plants that produce a few flowers every day for many weeks or months, and some that produce a lot of flowers over a short period of time.

Flowers for butterflies

You might think that only flowers specially adapted for butterflies would be suitable, but this is not the case. A very wide range of flowers, adapted for pollination by many different types of animal, can be used by butterflies, although they do not generally visit those of the orchid and pea families.

Most plant species that are adapted for butterfly pollination have small flowers, often crowded together in large inflorescences opening over a relatively long period of time. The individual flowers are not complicated in structure, but are usually trumpet-shaped with a tube of not more than a couple of centimetres (1in) in length, because the proboscis of butterflies is not as long as that of many moths or the tongues of hummingbirds.

Although some butterfly flowers are sweetly scented, this does not seem to be essential, because butterflies will visit flowers that have little scent. Similarly, it is often said that butterflies prefer bluish flowers, while birds go for red ones, but again butterflies will visit flowers of a variety of colours, although it is true that some species seem to prefer one colour over another.

Those who like to attract butterflies into their gardens will know that the various species and cultivars of buddleia will bring in large numbers of butterflies when they are in flower. Most of the outdoor buddleias are unfortunately not suitable for the living tropical greenhouse, because they cannot cope with the moist, hot conditions without becoming susceptible to pests. They also have a rather short flowering period which means that most of the time they will be taking up valuable space without providing any benefits.

A monarch butterfly taking advantage of the ideal flower structure of a buddleia.

Some of the tenderer types, such as *Buddleia fellowiana* are more suitable, provided you can keep them small enough with careful pruning or by growing them in a small pot, which restricts the roots.

Two flowering plants stand out as the most frequently grown in a living tropical greenhouse. These are lantanas, which belong to the family Verbenaceae, and pentas, which belong to the Rubiaceae. Both of these families are worth bearing in mind when looking for flowers that will provide nectar for your butterflies. Regardless of what type of growth habit they show, plant species that are in the same family will have flowers constructed along the same lines, because that is the way botanists classify their plants. Both lantanas and pentas produce flowers over a very long period, even up to 12 months. Both may grow too well and need replacing from time to time and both come in a variety of colours and growth habits.

A third plant that is likely to be in every living tropical greenhouse is *Asclepias curassavica*, belonging to the family Asclepiadaceae. It is a weed in many tropical countries, having seeds that are carried by a rosette of long hairs and which are easily set and germinate well. The flowers are attractive and specially adapted for pollination by butterflies: they trap the insect by a leg while it is eating. It doesn't hurt them; after some vigorous flapping, even a small heliconid butterfly can break free and visit another flower. This plant is also a larval foodplant for several species of danaid butterflies.

One or two vigorous climbers in the genus *Psiguria*, from the Cucurbitaceae family, are highly desirable if heliconid butterflies are present, because they also flower over a period of months with each inflorescence producing just a few flowers each day.

Some books name the flowers that tropical butterflies like to visit, but it is often difficult to obtain these plants, because they are not commonly in cultivation. Local plant nurseries may have many other possible nectar plants for sale, but not all of these plants can cope with the conditions in the greenhouse. They may have been

Lantana camara *is a must for the living tropical greenhouse, but remember that the attractive black berries are poisonous to humans.*

treated with insecticides, but it seems that the nectar from insecticide-sprayed plants is not so lethal as are the leaves to larvae, but take care.

In the wild, plants have flowers that are almost entirely of the form known as 'single', but in cultivation, plants with 'double' flowers are extremely common. Although there are many different types of double flower, most have modifications which make it more difficult for butterflies to obtain nectar from them. Some also have stamens – the structures involved in the production of the pollen so essential to the heliconid butterflies – that are modified into extra petals and do not produce pollen. For choice, always go for a 'single-flowered' variety.

Plants for the larvae

While a few of the nectar plants may also be used as foodplants by the larvae – the asclepiads and border bananas are good examples – it is necessary to grow many plants just as larval food. In the next chapter some of the plant families and a few individual species are briefly mentioned. Those butterfly books that give useful information on the biology of tropical butterflies will give lists of the plants that the larvae have been reported feeding on, generally in their natural habitats. Some of the plants named may have been incorrectly identified; other books mention only a genus of plants, leaving you to guess which of the many species in the genus is the foodplant. And just because you can get the particular plant

The common blue passion flower is a useful larval foodplant for heliconids and can survive outdoors in many sheltered places.

species that is mentioned, doesn't mean the larvae are going to eat it. What's more, the adult butterflies may decline to lay their ova on it. This may be because there are several genetically different strains of the butterfly, or because the

butterfly has a preference for the foodplant it enjoyed as a larvae. Very little is known about this aspect of the life of tropical butterflies. Take note also that there are often various strains of a plant species and that plants have their names changed as often, if not more so, than butterflies.

Plants that are going to be larval foodplants must be well grown before they are used and you will need a substantial supply of them. The stress endured by a plant when its soft young leaves are eaten is serious and a well-established root system is needed to cope with this. Remember also that when a young bud has been eaten, another will not appear in its place, because buds normally only arise in the angle between a leaf and a stem. If you are unfamiliar with the nature of plant growth, you may find a book on the basics useful.

Passion flowers are essential if heliconid butterflies are present. *Passiflora* is an extremely complicated genus of plants. You should double-check any passion flowers you buy in garden centres, because these plants are often wrongly labelled. It is something of a personal choice which of the many species you plant, but we suggest *Passiflora auriculata*, *P. biflora*, *P. caerulea*, *P. manicata*, *P. rubra* and *P. vitifolia* for a start. The various species of passion flower need, or tolerate, different conditions. Very few are tolerant of frost and even these may be killed to ground level.

Although they are more sub-tropical than tropical, every living tropical greenhouse needs some plants from the rue family (Rutaceae). Many species of swallowtails from the tropics have larvae that eat these, while others use plants from the Aristolochiaceae. Plants in the genera *Citrus* and *Fortunella* are usually expensive to purchase and take a long time to reach a good size when grown

Passiflora biflora *produces pairs of small but attractive flowers. Its leaves are the preferred food of some heliconid larvae.*

from seeds. Although they are evergreen, this does not mean that they produce new leaves all the year round. Most are grafted on to rootstocks rather than grown from seed. Kumquats (*Fortunella* species) produce small edible fruit, and leaves that are not as tough as those of lemon or orange. You should expect any citrus plants that you buy to contain systemic insecticides used against scale insects. Related plants in the same family, such as *Choisya ternata* and *Ruta graveolens* are frost hardy and are tolerated by some swallowtail larvae. *Poncirus trifoliata* is another hardy but very spiny member of the family, but it is deciduous and does not take easily to tropical greenhouse conditions.

The family Asclepiadaceae shows great differences between its genera and species in both flowers and plant form. There is a strong association between this family of plants and the danaid group of butterflies. Biochemicals from asclepiads and other plants are essential for the successful mating of many danaids. The tropical

weed *Asclepias curassavica* grows well in a greenhouse, while some members of the same genus can be grown outdoors in temperate climates. *Danaus plexippus* (the monarch) is a large butterfly with larvae that eat a lot, so plenty of plants are necessary for this and other danaids.

Banana plants are the very essence of the tropics and some are readily available to the gardener. Unless the greenhouse is very tall, it is best to avoid those with edible bananas, because they will grow far too large, even when described as 'dwarf' (*Musa cavendishii*). It is worth remembering that some plants are genetically dwarf, because they lack the hormone that makes them grow tall, but others may be temporarily dwarf because they have been treated with an anti-hormone. The so-called 'border' bananas (*Musa velutina* and other species) are small, and although they do not produce edible bananas, their flowers are attractive and the fruit, which are small and pink, do contain seeds from which new plants can be grown. Any 'stems' (the stem is actually a mass of sheathing leaf stalks) that have flowered die back to the ground, sometimes to be replaced with suckers from the base. Alternatively, new plants can be grown from seed. Border bananas can be grown in pots or in the soil and the leaves can grow large but remain fairly soft. This is a good thing, because bananas are one of the foodplants for the larvae of giant owl butterflies (*Caligo* species).

There are actually very few plants that are not the foodplant of some species of butterfly or moth, but it may prove very difficult, if not impossible, to obtain the livestock that would eat them. At other times it may be that they are quite unsuitable for your conditions. Among the plants whose leaves are eaten by relatively easily obtained butterfly larvae are *Dipteracanthus* (=*Ruellia*) species and *Perilepta* (=*Strobilanthus*) species, both from the Acanthaceae. Oleanders, cassias and spider flowers (*Cleome spinosa*) are all useful additions to the living tropical greenhouse for the same reason.

In time you will no doubt house other plants because they are attractive for one reason or another or because they were gifts from others

Edible bananas are dramatic, but grow too large before they fruit to be useful in a small greenhouse.

In addition to the main vista, it is always desirable to have a place devoted to the propagation of the plants that your butterflies need, because replacements will be needed from time to time.

Now we feel bound to add a word of caution for those who may let enthusiasm overtake knowledge. Some of the plants that can be grown in a living tropical greenhouse, just as in an ordinary greenhouse or garden, can be harmful to humans, because they are poisonous. Some butterflies, such as the heliconids and pipevine swallowtails, store the poisons from their foodplants to make themselves unpalatable to predators. Berries, such as those of lantanas, can look good to us, but are also poisonous. Other plants can cause skin rashes if you come into contact with their leaves or juice. It is well known, for example, that contact with rue leaves, followed by exposure to sunlight, can cause blistering of the skin. Never eat anything that you do not know for certain is edible, and use gloves when cutting down plants that have got out of control. If you do not already know about such things, you should study a book that deals with the topic.

Some plant families contain many species that are harmful to humans. You should expect any plant you do not know in the families Apocynaceae, Asclepiadaceae, Euphorbiaceae, Ranunculaceae and Solanaceae to be harmful. This does not mean that all the plants in the other families are not harmful. Even some which we generally think of as containing edible plants may also contain some posionous species. The pea family (Papilionaceae=Leguminosae), for example, also contains the extremely poisonous rosary pea (*Abrus precatorius*).

Some plants that are commonly grown in tropical greenhouses, especially those described as 'rainforests' belong to families that are not of particular interest to someone who is breeding butterflies. Typical examples of this are species in the family Araceae. Many have large leaves, often attractive shapes and variegations, but butterflies whose larvae use such plants are rarely available. Most aroids grow well in quite low light levels

who thought you might like them. Space is the main thing which restricts what you can grow, as well as the conditions you are able to create. Some plants may only be temporary residents, brought in for their flowers although they may not be able to cope, in the long term, with the conditions. The art, as opposed to the craft, of the living tropical greenhouse is to make it an attractive place to be, even for those who do not at first share your enthusiasm for all the plants and creatures that are contained in it.

and are not attacked by many pests, hence their obvious popularity with some horticulturalists.

Plant names

Before mentioning some particular plants in the next chapter, it is worth pausing to consider the complications of getting the names right. For many readers this is perhaps one of the most puzzling and aggravating aspects. There are many reasons why names need to be changed, and various learned committees spend their time trying to bring order to chaos, following rules set out in

The aroid Epipremnum aureum *was known as* Scindapsis aureus. *It is usually grown as a small house plant, but can grow very large in a tropical greenhouse.*

the two relevant International Codes of Nomenclature. The easiest reference source for the gardener is, perhaps, the UK's *RHS* (Royal Horticultural Society) *Plant Finder*, in whatever is the most recent edition. The plant names listed in that book, covering many tens of thousands of plants which are available from listed nurseries in the UK, are based on the RHS's version of the computer database BG-BASE (TM). It is their aim to make the RHS horticultural database the most comprehensive and thoroughly checked database of its kind in the world.

You should remember, however, that it will not help you, or anyone else, to identify a plant, but it will enable the currently appropriate version of its name to be used once you have correctly identified it. The name of a plant is not a characteristic of the plant but simply a reasonably convenient peg on which we humans can hang all the information that has been collected about it. If this peg is the wrong one or we don't know it then information cannot be properly stored, retrieved or transmitted to others. Provided they can be cross-referenced, previously used names (synonyms) need not be a problem for those who consult books that have not just been published using the latest concensus of information. Unfortunately, it is in the correct identification of a plant in the first instance, to any one of its alternative names, that most of the problems lie for the living tropical greenhouse gardener. There is no universally accepted definition of what constitutes a species and the criteria used to separate species are often things that are not readily visible in a photograph or drawing. We apologize to readers if any of the plants or animals mentioned in our book do not, at least, bear a name that is currently considered correct, or its synonym, and we do appreciate that for the sake of familiarity we have used some older synonyms.

5 Plants for paradise

There are many books dealing with the plants that ordinary gardeners grow in their greenhouses or conservatories and also those grown by specialists of particular families or groups of plants. When setting up a living tropical greenhouse, you will have to search out information from all kinds of sources. You may often need to find out about plants that are comparatively rare in cultivation in temperate climates, although they may be common enough in tropical regions.

In many ways, this is the situation that faced gardeners in the early days of plant exploration, when many new species were being brought back from far-away places, but nobody knew the best conditions to grow them in. It may seem strange to ordinary gardeners that this chapter is set out as an alphabetical arrangement of plant families, but this is the way that those setting up a living tropical greenhouse will have to go about things. For a particular named plant that you come across for the first time, you will want to know what family it belongs to. Then you can start to track down something of its biology and other plants that are related to it and so, perhaps, deduce the sort of conditions under which it will grow successfully.

If you are lucky, a useful starting place for this information would be a large general plant text. General greenhouse books usually have little of interest for a tropical greenhouse, but a good conservatory book will yield useful cultural information, as will some good houseplant books. Unfortunately, the owner

Oleander is a valuable plant in the greenhouse, both for its flowers and leaves which are a larval foodplant for some danaids.

of a living tropical greenhouse often finds that the plants mentioned in butterfly books are not in the gardening books.

The first step then is to find out what family the plant belongs to. Your attention must then turn to truly botanical texts. Knowing the family is a great help, because you can then get a general idea of the type of plants in the family. If you cannot obtain one species, it is sometimes worth trying another related one on the assumption, not always correct, that plants in the same family are more likely to be suitable as butterfly foodplants than those in different families.

The following brief descriptions give some idea of the families and plants that are often found in a living tropical greenhouse. As is so often the case, the number of genera and species in a family cannot be stated precisely, so the numbers quoted should be considered as reasonable indications only. We cannot give cultural information in such a small book as this and refer our readers to the many gardening books that are available for details of the commonly cultivated plants. There are, of course, many families that are not listed below, most containing foodplants for tropical butterflies that are also not discussed in this book. We hope that our readers will be inspired to start the search for, and undoubtedly contribute to, the knowledge about both the plants and the butterflies. It is worth remembering that plants are classified largely on the details of their flower structure and not on their leaf shape or form. A single genus may contain plants from many different environments and countries in the world and the species can look and be biochemically very different from one another.

The ease with which plants can be obtained varies from country to country. Joining a local club or society with specific interests in breeding tropical butterflies, or insects in general, may be a starting point. Companies selling 'exotic' seeds, or plant societies with worldwide membership (such as those for passion flowers) is another approach. Local directories of plant sources will give details of nurseries, and nurseries usually have their own lists. Plant names may not always be right.

Strobilanthes dyeriana *has attractive multicoloured leaves and grows well in a tropical greenhouse.*

ACANTHACEAE

Most of the 2,500 or so species in the 250 genera are tropical shrubs; only a few are from temperate regions. Several species are cultivated as ornamentals; many are familiar indoor plants. The flowers are attractive to look at, but not usually suitable as sources of nectar for butterflies, although the leaves of some are larval foodplants for some nymphalids. There have been several changes of the generic names of some species.

Ruellia (=Dipteracanthus) *makoyana* is the most commonly available of the five species in the genus and is a larval foodplant for some *Precis* (=Junonia) species.

Strobilanthes (=Perilepta) *dyeriana* is one of some 250 species in the genus. It is a larval foodplant for some *Precis* (=Junonia) species.

Thunbergia alata is an attractive climbing plant and a familiar species from among the 250 or so in the genus.

ANNONACEAE

A family of mainly tropical plants, with about 2,000 species in some 120 genera. Most are trees or shrubs.

Annona squamosa, the custard apple, and a few others of the 100 or so species in the genus are commonly cultivated for their edible fruit, and seeds can be obtained from them. The leaves are the main foodplant for *Graphium agamemnon*.

APOCYNACEAE

This large family has some 1,500 species spread over about 180 genera. Most are tropical plants and the species range from small perennial herbs, through shrubs and climbers to some of the tall trees of tropical rainforests.

Tweedia caerulea is a climber. Its flowers, which are attractive to butterflies, are produced over many months and followed by elongated pods.

Nerium oleander is the most commonly grown of the three species in the genus and there are several cultivated forms, some with double flowers. They are grown not only for the flowers, but also for the fact that some danaid butterflies use them as a larval foodplant.

ARISTOLOCHIACEAE

A family of mainly tropical, but with some temperate, species; in all about 620 in some seven genera. Most are twining climbers with main stems that become woody.

Aristolochia species (of which there are some 500) differ considerably in leaf shape and flower size, but are generally known as Dutchman's pipes. The flowers mostly emit a strong and unpleasant odour. The leaves are the food for larvae of many Old and New World species of papilionids.

ASCLEPIADACEAE

There are between 1,800 and 2,000 species in this family, spread over about 250 genera. Most are tropical or subtropical plants with a milky sap and there are representatives of perennial herbs, shrubs, climbers and trees. Some species are succulents and many are grown as ornamentals. The family has a close relationship with the danaid butterflies and provides many larval foodplants. In some genera the flowers are specially adapted for insect pollination: they trap the insect by the leg or proboscis while transferring a waxy mass of pollen on to its body.

Araujia sericofera is a frequently mentioned twining climber that will catch moths by the proboscis, but it does not always let them go. It can serve as a larval foodplant.

Asclepias curassavica is the most commonly cultivated member from around 120 species in the genus. It is a larval foodplant for several danaid butterflies and the flowers are attractive as nectar sources and will grip the legs of heliconids for a few seconds. Its seeds are readily set.

Tweedia caerulea may be the only species in the genus. It is a climber with blue flowers. These are very attractive to butterflies and the leaves act as a larval foodplant.

Tylophora species from among the 50 or so in the genus are foodplants for various danaid butterflies. They are twining climbers.

ASTERACEAE (=COMPOSITAE)

The 25,000 or so species in this family are ascribed to about 1,100 genera. Members of the family are found throughout the world and all manner of life-forms are found, from herbaceous annuals, biennials and perennials to evergreen shrubs. There are a few climbers, some succulents and even species that reach tree-like proportions despite being herbaceous. There are many cultivated plants in the family and many cultivated forms. The flowers of most are attractive to insects, including butterflies. Not all of the commonly cultivated garden flowers are able to stand the conditions in a tropical greenhouse.

Cinerarias are useful flowering pot plants to bring in for the winter. The one shown here is providing nectar for the swallowtail Papilio dardanus.

Ageratum species and their cultivated forms from among the 60 or so species generally have bluish flowers that are useful nectar sources, especially for glasswings.

Argyranthemum (=part of *Chrysanthemum*) species and cultivars, such as 'Yellow Star', flower for many weeks and some cope well with the conditions in a tropical greenhouse, providing nectar for butterflies.

Aster species (of which there are some 500), and the many cultivated forms, are usually too tall for the greenhouse, but dwarf forms are worth growing because they will flower early under warm conditions and Michaelmas daisies, for example, are well-known for attracting butterflies.

Coreopsis species are worth considering as sources of nectar. There are some 120 species in the genus.

Euryops pectinatus has bright yellow flowers that are useful sources of nectar and the plant does quite well in the greenhouse.

Liatris spicata is an interesting plant that copes well in the greenhouse, producing a mass of grass-

Senecio confusus *produces dramatic flowers that butterflies visit for nectar.*

like leaves and a tall spike of bluish flowers that open over a long period of time. There are some 40 species in the genus.

Senecio confusus is a dramatic climber from a genus with thousands of species. The brilliant orange flowers are borne twice a year and are very attractive to butterflies. The plant is susceptible to both high and low temperatures and you should take care to place it in a suitable site in the greenhouse. Bundles of plants of the common, temperate-zone weed *Senecio vulgaris*, and possibly other species, are a useful source of biochemicals for many danaid and some ithomiid adult butterflies.

Tithonia *species produce large, bright flowers over many weeks and are easily grown from seed.*

Tagetes species and cultivated forms are readily available, but most will not tolerate moist conditions above about 30°C (86°F) and so need to be planted in cooler, drier, places in the greenhouse. They are a useful nectar source from a genus with about 50 species.

Tithonia rotundifolia is one of about 10 species in a genus which has flowers that are very attractive to butterflies and produced over a long period of time. They are like very large and brightly coloured daisies, and are just as attractive to gardeners.

BALSAMINACEAE

There are only four genera in this family, but up to about 600 species, from tropical and temperate regions. They are annual or perennial herbs.

Impatiens walleriana (=*sultani*) is the most frequently cultivated member of its genus, which contains the majority of the species in the family and some hybrids. It is cultivated for its flowers, which are attractive to look at, coming in many different colour forms, and provide nectar for some of the larger butterflies.

BORAGINACEAE

The 100 or so genera in this family contain some 2,000 species in all. They are mostly plants of temperate or subtropical regions and the family includes herbs, shrubs, trees and a few climbers. The flowers are mostly pollinated by insects and some are very attractive to butterflies.

Echium species vary considerably in size but the flowers of most of the 40 species are attractive to butterflies. They are annual or biennial herbs.

Heliotropium species are well-known garden plants whose flowers are visited by many butterflies. Biochemicals contained in the plants are also important for the successful breeding of many danaid species although the larvae do not eat the leaves.

Heliotropes are readily available and provide masses of flowers for months if carefully tended.

BROMELIACEAE

The 50 or so genera in this family contain about 2,000 species. Most are tropical or warm temperate plants with a basal rosette of leaves borne on a short stem. Many are familiar houseplants and some have water reservoirs (tanks) at the base of the leaves which trap rain water. The inflorescence usually arises from the centre of the rosette and after flowering the rosette dies and is replaced by suckers arising from it. The cultivated forms mostly have tough leaves and the plants are grown for their attractive flowers or coloured leaves. The flowers may act as a nectar source for some butterflies.

Aechmea fasciata is commonly available as a pot plant from among the 150 or so species in the genus.

Ananas comosus, the pineapple, is the most readily available of the five species in the genus. It can be grown easily by rooting the leafy top of the edible fruit, but it is slow to flower.

CANNACEAE

The single genus in this family contains about 30 species, but there are many cultivated forms and hybrids. The leaf stalks sheathe the stem, which rises from swollen underground rhizomes. The flowers are very attractive and the leaves are a useful larval food for some brassolids.

Canna indica and its many forms is the species usually seen in greenhouses. It provides dramatic colour as well as soft leaves that are eaten by larvae of *Caligo* species.

The spider flower, Cleome spinosa, *grows rapidly from seed and the flowers are produced in sequence while the leaves are eaten by some pierid larvae.*

CAPPARIDACEAE

A family of tropical and subtropical plants with around 700 species in up to 50 genera, containing herbs, shrubs, trees and a few climbers.

Cleome spinosa is commonly grown in tropical greenhouses as a foodplant for the larvae of various pierids. The plant has a strong odour when touched and a scattering of short, stout

Bryophyllum species (20 or so) tend to grow rather lush and need supporting, but they make an attractive feature. Some species produce adventitious plantlets from the edges of the leaves.

Kalanchoe blossfeldiana is commonly available as a pot plant (from some 200 species in the genus) and provides useful flowers when others are in short supply. The conditions required for subsequent flowering are not always easy to obtain in a tropical greenhouse, but the plants will grow on for some time.

Sedum spectabile is a commonly cultivated member of a genus with about 600 species. Outside it flowers in autumn, but potted plants can be stimulated into earlier flowering if they are brought into the greenhouse. The flowers are very attractive to butterflies.

CUCURBITACEAE
There are about 700 species in the family, distributed over some 90 genera. The majority are climbing plants.

Psiguria species produce flowers over a period of many weeks, and they are very attractive to heliconid butterflies. Although they are rather difficult to obtain, there should be at least one in every living tropical greenhouse. The plants take some time to establish and may produce a substantial amount of leaf before they flower. They produce separate male and female flowers.

EUPHORBIACEAE
This family has some 5,000 species, spread over about 300 genera. Most are tropical plants, but some species are found in the temperate zone.

Euphorbia milii (=*splendens*) is a succulent plant with upright spiny stems that frequently branch. It requires care with the water supply if it is to retain its leaves, but it produces flowers over a long period. The coloured bracts attract butterflies to the flowers and the plant is grown as a source of nectar. The genus contains about 2,000 species. Some are herbaceous, others are shrubs.

Heliconid butterflies find the flowers of Psiguria *species irresistible and often compete for the one or two that open each day.*

spines. The pink or whitish flowers are attractive and unusual in shape, giving rise to the common name of spider flower. This is the only species out of around 150 that is readily available for cultivation and it sets seed readily.

COMPOSITAE see ASTERACEAE

CRASSULACEAE
A family of some 1,500 species spread through about 35 genera. The majority of these succulent plants are herbs, but there are some shrubby species. Some grow well in a tropical greenhouse and will produce flowers that are attractive to butterflies. Most tolerate dry conditions.

Jatropha podagrica is a succulent plant with a short stem that is swollen at the base. At the top it bears a rosette of large leaves and produces a small, but stout, branching inflorescence. The flowers are attractive to butterflies and the plant is grown as a nectar source. The leaves fall off under dry conditions. There are about 175 species in the genus.

FABACEAE (=LEGUMINOSAE)

This is one of the largest families, with over 17,000 species in about 700 genera. All types of plants occur, from herbs, shrubs and trees to climbers, and from desert to aquatic habitats.

Cassia species, of which there may be as many as 600, are mainly tropical or warm temperate plants. They are grown as the larval foodplants for many species of pierids.

Mucuna species (some 120 are described) are among the many members of the family that are foodplants for morpho butterflies. They are rather difficult to obtain and some species have stinging hairs on the seed pods.

GESNERIACEAE

A family with some 2,000 species in about 125 genera. Most are tropical herbs or shrubs and many are cultivated as ornamentals, with numerous named cultivars. Although they make attractive indoor plants, the flowers are not particularly useful as nectar sources.

Cassias are grown for their leaves rather than their flowers. The leaves are food for some pierid larvae.

Saintpaulia ionantha grows well in a shady, warm spot and the single-flowered forms are useful for providing colour in the greenhouse. There are 12 species in the genus.

Streptocarpus saxorum is a good small plant to grow in a hanging basket. It produces lots of pale blue flowers that are borne well clear of the leaves on long slender stalks and which are visited by some butterflies, as well as adding interest for the gardener and being easy to grow. The genus has some 100 or more species as well as many hybrids and cultivars.

LABIATAE see LAMIACEAE

LAMIACEAE (=LABIATAE)

There are some 3,000 species, spread over about 200 genera in this well-known family, which contains many cultivated plants. Most are herbs or small shrubs, and members of the family are found in all regions.

Coleus blumeii (=cultivars of *Solenostemon*) in its many cultivated forms is grown mostly for its variegated leaves, which are also a larval foodplant for the African *Precis* (=*Junonia*) *octavia*. The flowers provide nectar for butterflies and are produced over quite a long period of time.

LEGUMINOSAE see FABACEAE

LOGANIACEAE

This family of some 600 species, spread over about 30 genera, has representatives in temperate, subtropical and tropical regions. There are climbers, shrubs and trees.

Buddleia (or *Buddleja*) species, of which there are some 100 species, as well as hybrids and cultivated forms, are well known as nectar sources for butterflies. The main problem is their large size and rather limited period of flowering. Those that are fully hardy generally do not like the conditions in a tropical greenhouse for long periods. *B. fellowiana* is quite good, as is *B. madagascariensis*, but both grow very large and

The flowers of Buddleja madagascariensis *hang down and provide an ample supply of nectar. This plant is feeding* Idea leuconoe.

the hairs on the leaves and stems of the latter species can be an irritant to humans, especially when pruning old plants.

MALVACEAE
A family of some 80 genera and more than a 1,000 species. *Hibiscus rosa-sinensis* is found in most tropical greenhouses where its large and brightly coloured flowers are attractive both to the gardener and to some butterflies. It can grow very large and may require fairly frequent pruning.

MARANTACEAE
There are about 350 species of tropical herbaceous perennials, in some 30 genera, in this family. Many are grown as houseplants because of their attractively marked leaves. Some are alternative larval foodplants for some brassolids, but are not the preferred ones.

Calathea species are commonly available as houseplants and make attractive, low-growing plants for the tropical greenhouse given high humidity and shade. They will provide larval food for *Caligo* species in emergency situations, when other plants are not available.

MUSACEAE
There are some 40 species and very many cultivated forms between the two genera in this family of tropical plants. They are evergreen, perennial herbs, many of which grow very large. As larval foodplants for many of the brassolid butterflies, at least one member of this family is a must for the living tropical greenhouse. Most of the edible bananas grow to a very large size and take up a lot of space, even the 'dwarf' ones.

Musa velutina is a 'border' banana that grows to only a few feet in height and flowers easily within one year. The fruit are small, red and not edible. The plant also readily produces seeds and offsets to replace the main stem after it has flowered. All the leaves stay soft enough even for young larvae to eat, unlike those of the edible bananas, and little biomass is wasted in the thin 'stems' which are actually the leaf bases. The flowers are a source of nectar and pollen.

MYRTACEAE
A large family with around 3,000 species in about 100 genera, ranging from lax shrubs to very tall trees. The majority of species is from tropical or subtropical regions.

Leptospermum scoparium is a small shrubby plant that is grown for its flowers, which are very rich in nectar. There are some 50 species in the genus, in the Australasian region.

NYCTAGINACEAE

A family of mostly tropical herbs, shrubs and trees, with about 290 species in 30 genera.

Bougainvillea species, of which there are about 18, and various cultivated hybrids, are grown for the showy bracts that surround the much smaller flowers. They are visited for nectar by some butterflies, but are mostly more attractive to the gardener than to the butterflies.

ORCHIDACEAE

With some 18,000 species and about 750 genera, this family is one of the largest. It contains many visually spectacular plants and numerous cultivated forms and hybrids. Although of limited interest to the tropical butterfly greenhouse it may well be worth growing one or two of those that can stand the hot environment, if for no other reason than the fact that many of the tropical species, just like tropical butterflies, are threatened by habitat destruction.

Phalaenopsis species and forms are the most commonly available orchids that require the type of conditions found in the tropical greenhouse. They will produce attractive flowers but are of little use to the butterflies.

PALMAE (=ARECACEAE)

This family has about 2,800 species, spread over some 210 genera. Most are tropical or subtropical plants and a few are cultivated and have many distinct forms. Some small-growing species, and the young plants of others, are commonly available as house or conservatory plants. The leaves of some are larval foodplants for some tropical butterflies, but older leaves may become very tough and the growth of new leaves can be quite slow.

Cocos nucifera is often available as a young seedling pot plant and produces large but rather tough leaves. It is a larval foodplant for some butterflies, such as the brassolid *Opsiphanes cassina*. The growth form of *Syagrus* (=*Cocos*) *weddeliana* is very different, with small, soft, feathery leaves and when available this is much to be preferred for the tropical greenhouse. There are said to be some 50 species of *Syagrus*, but perhaps only one of *Cocos*.

Howeia (=*Kentia*) *forsteriana* is available as a pot plant. The leaves are quite soft and a suitable larval foodplant for *Elymnias hypermnestra*.

Phoenix dactylifera can be grown from the seeds of the edible date, but produces very tough and spiny leaves early in its life and can become a hazard in the greenhouse.

P. canariensis is a commonly available ornamental species from the 17 or so species in the genus and has much less spiny leaves. *P. roebelenii* is to be preferred when it is available.

The flowers of Leptospermum scoparium *are only produced over a short period of time, but they are extremely rich in nectar and butterflies love them.*

Passiflora alata *has heavy, fragrant flowers that are truly spectacular.*

Passiflora edulis *has large glossy leaves that can be used by a few heliconid larvae.*

PASSIFLORACEAE

A family of mainly tropical and subtropical plants with some 20 genera and around 600 species. Mostly they are climbers, but there are some shrubs, trees and herbs in the family.

Passiflora species are grown in all living tropical greenhouses, for the leaves form the larval foodplant of heliconid butterflies. The flowers of the various species differ very widely in appearance, although they all have a similar basic construction. Some butterflies will only lay ova on one or two species, but others will use a wide range of species. There are many cultivated hybrids and forms. The conditions required for good growth can differ between the species, so you should consider this before you make a purchase. Temperature range is important.

PLUMBAGINACEAE

A family with about 560 species of herbs, shrubs and climbers, in 10 genera.

Plumbago auriculata (=*capensis*) is the most widely cultivated member of the genus, which has some 12 species. It makes an attractive shrub for

the greenhouse gardener and its blue flowers are visited by some butterflies. However, the leaves are not the larval food of any commonly available butterfly.

PRIMULACEAE

This is a family with some 28 genera and around 1,000 species, mainly from temperate regions. Few can tolerate the conditions of a tropical greenhouse for long.

Primula obconica, when in flower, is a useful pot plant for providing nectar when other flowers are in short supply. It is one of the few species of *Primula* (out of some 500) that will tolerate heat, but unfortunately some people develop an allergy to certain strains of it.

RUBIACEAE

This is one of the largest families, with some 7,000 species in about 500 genera. Mostly they are tropical or subtropical shrubs or trees, but there are also many temperate zone herbaceous species. There are also many cultivated forms of many of the species. The flowers of many are good nectar sources for butterflies.

Bouvardia hybrids are the most frequently cultivated members of this genus of some 50 tropical species. The rather open, shrubby plants bear masses of small, but very attractive, white or coloured flowers and they are a useful nectar source.

Pentas lanceolata is an essential nectar source in any butterfly greenhouse. The masses of small flowers in rounded inflorescences are produced throughout the year and are very attractive to butterflies. There are several colour forms in cultivation, from white, through pink to brilliant red. The ordinary forms grow quite large in a greenhouse, but dwarf strains are available. The genus contains some 50 species.

RUTACEAE

There are some 900 species in this family, spread over 150 genera, and many cultivated hybrids among the citrus fruits. Most species are from warm-temperate or tropical climates.

Choisya ternata is the most readily available of the six species in this genus. Many tropical swallowtail larvae will eat the leaves and developing flowers, and because the species is hardy and evergreen it is a useful foodplant. However, it does not like being cultivated in a tropical greenhouse for long periods.

Citrus species and hybrids are important larval foodplants for many tropical swallowtail butterflies. They are generally rather slow growing and do not recover quickly from damage. Some will set seed easily and these can be germinated, but they will not flower for many years. Most commercially available plants are grafted on to rootstocks. There may be some 12 species in the genus but also many hybrids and cultivars.

Ruta graveolens will grow in a greenhouse and the rather flimsy leaves are eaten by the larvae of some tropical swallowtails. We do not recommend it, however, because some people develop severe skin reactions if they brush against it with bare skin which is then exposed to bright sunlight.

Passiflora oerstedii *has rather small, pale flowers, but it is one of many good plants for the living tropical greenhouse. Some heliconid larvae eat the leaves.*

STRELITZIACEAE

This small family of some 55 species in four genera consists of tropical plants that are known mostly as ornamentals. The leaves of some are alternative larval foodplants for some brassolids but they are generally much tougher than those of *Musa* species.

Strelitzia reginae and others of the four species in this genus are so striking when in flower that they have earned the name 'bird of paradise' flowers. Butterflies find the flowers a rich source of nectar, but the plant is rather slow growing and needs quite a lot of room in relation to its value to the butterfly breeder.

VERBENACEAE

This large family, of some 3,000 species spread over about 75 genera, contains herbs, shrubs, trees and climbers. A number of species are cultivated as ornamentals and their flowers are usually attractive to butterflies.

Although eaten by some swallowtail larvae, rue is not recommended in a tropical greenhouse because accidental contact with it can cause dermatitis.

SOLANACEAE

This is a very large family of up to 3,000 species in about 90 genera but with many cultivated species and forms. Most are herbs, but there are some climbers, shrubs and trees and many are poisonous. Some are foodplants for ithomiid and other butterflies.

Brunfelsia pauciflora (=*calycina*) is commonly grown as an indoor plant and has large, attractive flowers which change colour as they age.

Cestrum species are foodplants for the larvae of butterflies of the genus *Greta*. *Cestrum nocturnum* is a greenhouse shrub with attractive flowers, and shrubby species such as *C. parquii* will retain their leaves over the winter inside. There are some 150 species in the genus.

Clerodendrum species are commonly grown in greenhouses, but only a few of the 400 or so species in the genus are available. Most are tropical or subtropical plants and the flowers of many are attractive.

Lantana camara is found in most butterfly greenhouses and produces a sequence of flowers that are attractive to butterflies over a period of many months. It should be noted that the attractive black berries are poisonous. There are some 150 species in the genus.

Stachytarpheta species produce long spikes of flowers that open sequentially over a period of many weeks and are attractive to many butterflies. There are about 100 species in the genus. Some, such as *S. mutabilis*, grow quite tall with

Cestrum parquii *is an excellent larval foodplant for the glasswing (*Greta oto*) and will keep its leaves all winter under cover.*

substantial inflorescences of small reddish flowers that open sequentially over a long period. Others, such as *S. indica*, are smaller and have an inflorescence of very small blue flowers produced a few at a time, again for many days.

Verbena species and hybrids are widely available and the flowers of most are attractive to butterflies. There are about 250 species in the genus and many are well worth trying in the greenhouse.

ZINGIBERACEAE

There are some 1,300 species, in about 49 genera in this family of tropical plants. Herbaceous shoots arise from fleshy underground rhizomes and there are many cultivated species and selected forms. The leaves of some are an alternative larval foodplant for some brassolids.

Hedychium coronarium and other species and cultivated forms have dramatic flowers, which give rise to the common name of ginger lilies. Most of them are strongly scented. There are some 50 species in the genus. The leaves are eaten by the larvae of *Caligo* species, but the adults do not usually lay ova on the plant. Also, larval development may be slower than on *Musa* species.

Zingiber officinale is the edible ginger. Plants can be grown from fresh rhizomes bought in food shops, but they are not as attractive as the ginger lilies and are more valuable as a topic of conversation than as a part of the living tropical greenhouse. The genus contains some 80 or more species.

Hedychium speciosum, *one of the attractive ginger lilies.*

6 Foes and friends of the plants

Even the tough-looking leaves of passion flowers, such as those of Passiflora x belotii can be damaged if you wash them.

Once a suitable environment has been created, the breeder of tropical butterflies still has a number of problems to overcome. Firstly, the plants have to be kept healthy and growing. This is not just a question of nutrition and conditions, because plants are subject to numerous pests and diseases and many of these will thrive particularly well in a heated greenhouse. Ordinary gardeners often turn to pesticides, but these, even if they are 'organic' (in the sense of being derived from natural sources) cannot be used, because they will also harm the butterflies. Fortunately, a number of biological control agents are available.

Secondly, all stages of the butterfly life-cycle must also be protected from the predators, parasitoids and diseases that afflict them. In older literature, the reader may find the term parasite used rather than parasitoid. The difference is that parasites do not directly kill their hosts, but parasitoids do. Most of the problem creatures that the butterfly breeder will meet are killers.

Predators do not live in or on their prey, but lead totally independent lives. Some of the creatures that the ordinary gardener calls friends, such as spiders and ground beetles, are definitely enemies to the butterfly breeder.

At this point, it is worth drawing attention to what ecologists call 'population dynamics'. All the creatures that the butterfly breeder will either introduce or have in the greenhouse already have the potential to increase their numbers very rapidly. In some cases this is due to their high fecundity (that is, each female lays a lot of ova or has a lot of young), and in others to an ability to pass quickly through the life-cycle so that many generations can occur in a single year. If both of these features are present, there will be serious problems. If a female lays, say, 100 ova during her life and they all survive, the second generation will have 5,000 individuals, assuming that only half of the offspring are females. In the third generation there will be 250,000. Very soon the greenhouse will be overflowing with these creatures. Obviously this does not happen, because not all of the potential offspring reach maturity. This is due to the action of 'mortality factors', which cause the death of some of the offspring, and these factors will obviously be cumulative throughout the life-cycle. When we are using a biological control agent (i.e. another living organism) to control the numbers of a pest species, it is obvious that the pest must be present first, otherwise there will be no food for the control agent. Also, the numbers of the pest will build up first, to be followed by those of the control agent. This leads to an oscillation of the numbers of both organisms and all manner of things will influence how well the control agent works in the greenhouse.

From time to time, the suppliers of biological control agents introduce new organisms. It should be remembered that these are unlikely to have been tested in a butterfly greenhouse, so you should take care when trying them out: they may also attack some stages of the butterfly's life-cycle. If this were the case, they would prove very difficult to eliminate from the greenhouse. The control agents that are mentioned below have been used in butterfly greenhouses.

Problems with the plants

At the first sign of a pest attack, there are simple measures you can take. You can use your hands to remove one or two individuals. A paint brush dipped in methylated spirit is an old method of treating small outbreaks, particularly of mealy bugs and scale insects. If there are no butterfly

ova or larvae present, then leaves may be dipped or washed over with a solution of a few drops of washing-up liquid in tepid water. Some plants, such as *Asclepias* species and the tougher leaves of the citrus type, tolerate this well, but others, such as many *Passiflora* species, are very sensitive and therefore should not be washed over. In any case, this should not be done when the sun is shining directly on to the plant.

It is worth remembering that 'biofriendly' pest control materials are generally also lethal to butterfly ova and larvae, so you must read the fine print on the labels very carefully if you decide to use them. Biological control agents of the types mentioned below are generally even more sensitive to pesticides than the pests themselves.

There is also no reason why the 'natural' or 'organic' pest control sprays should be any less toxic to butterflies than the 'synthetic' ones. After all many of the most poisonous substances known come from plants.

Passiflora foetida is usually pest free because it has millions of small sticky hairs on it. However, it smells rather odd and few butterfly larvae will feed on it.

Pests

Once pests have been introduced into the greenhouse it is difficult to get rid of them, so the first rule is to put only clean plants into the greenhouse. This is not at all easy, because although you can see the adults of many pests, the ova and younger stages may be so small as to be hardly visible to the naked eye. If possible, any plants you obtain should be placed in a 'quarantine' propagator for a few weeks so that any pests present can develop to a visible size.

One way to check for pests is to take a piece of clear sticky tape (such as Sellotape) and brush the sticky side over the lower surfaces of the leaves. Tiny pests will stick to it and the tape can be examined with the help of a hand lens or low-powered microscope. It is quite difficult to distinguish friends from foes or from 'neutral creatures' that do no serious harm. Plants that

have been grown with only biological controls are more likely to be harbouring pests than those treated with pesticides.

Unfortunately, plants that have been treated with pesticides, especially those that have been treated with systemic insecticides (which get inside the plant and move to the growing tips), will need many months of further growth before they can be used in the butterfly greenhouse. Watch out also for potting composts that have pesticides already in them. It cannot, of course, be assumed that a plant which has pests on it has not been sprayed, because many pests have become resistant to pesticides and may flourish even on treated plants. In general, plants from temperate regions are more likely to become infested in a living tropical greenhouse than are genuine tropical plants, which are better adapted to the conditions.

When using biological control agents in the greenhouse, it should be remembered that they only survive when the appropriate pest is present. If, however, the pest has increased to a large extent, it will take a considerable time for the biological control agent to exert a significant control. During this time the pest may do quite a lot of damage. In addition, the fecundity and rate of growth of the pest and its control agent will probably be affected differently by temperature, humidity and daylength. The following short paragraphs are intended only as a brief introduction to the subject of biological control agents.

Aphids

There are many species of aphid and it is not practical for the butterfly breeder to attempt to identify the species that is present. The plants may not be the original hosts for the aphids, but because the conditions in the tropical greenhouse are very favourable, aphids, like all other pests, are likely to thrive. Some plants will be more or less free from aphid attack, pipevines (*Aristolochia* species) are an example, while others, members of the family Asclepiadaceae for example, may be heavily infested.

Two control agents are widely available for aphids. *Aphidoletes aphidimyza* is a tiny fly, the adult of which feeds on the honeydew secreted by

The poisonous pipevines, *such as this* Aristolochia grandiflora, *are resistant to most pests.*

There are many different species of aphid and they can do considerable damage to plants.

Leaf and plant hoppers

Like their close relatives, the aphids, leaf and plant hoppers suck the sap from plants. Outdoors, in temperate zone gardens, they do not usually cause serious damage, but in the living tropical greenhouse they can cause much harm. Not only do they weaken plants by taking sap, but the numerous feeding sites develop into pale whitish blotches, which in severe infestations can destroy a leaf. The adults of most species are a few millimetres in length. Their wings are folded along the back and they have the ability to leap rapidly from the leaf when approached. Unfortunately, there is no biological control available at the time of writing this book and, as always, you are well advised to check any plants that you bring into the greenhouse to prevent the hoppers' entry.

Mealy bugs

There are many species of mealy bugs, but the one most commonly found in the tropical greenhouse has a pinkish body and although it is an insect it looks like a tiny woodlouse. This can only be seen when the fluffy white 'wool' (really a waxy material) is scraped away. In fact these creatures are the females; the males are tiny, short-lived, winged insects that are rarely seen. The females lay a number of eggs close by and then die.

aphids. At this stage it only lives for just over a week, but the mated females will lay over a hundred ova close to colonies of aphids. The larvae that hatch from these ova attack and kill the aphids, finally sucking out the body fluids. The larvae are bright orange and can be seen quite easily, but the adults are rarely visible and most people would not recognize them.

The second control agent is *Aphidius matricariae*, a tiny parasitoid wasp. The female lays a single ovum inside an aphid. The ovum hatches into a larva that eats the inside of the aphid before cutting its way out and attaching the empty aphid skin to the leaf as a shelter in which to pupate. The aphid remains are called 'mummies' and can be seen quite easily, because they remain stuck to the leaves when other living aphids have moved away.

The pale white blotches are the feeding sites of hoppers. The insects jump away when you try to pick them off.

Verbena bonariensis has flowers that butterflies like, but in the greenhouse it is very susceptible to pests such as whiteflies.

Woolly masses containing many insects build up and are clearly visible. Often they are at the joints where the leaves are attached to the stems. They can soon spread out of control and seriously damage plants such as passion flowers.

The most commonly available biological control agent is a ladybird called *Cryptolaemus montrouziere*. The adult is brownish with a distinct orange tip at the end of its wing-cases. Its life-cycle is similar to the familiar spotted ladybirds. Mated females lay several hundred ova in a lifetime. Each ovum is laid into a mass of mealy bugs and hatches into a nymph which, like the adults, is a predator of mealy bugs.

Adult and young nymphs of *Cryptolaemus montrouziere* prefer ova and small mealy bugs, but the older nymphs will tackle any size of mealy bug. It takes a little practice to distinguish young ladybird nymphs from the mealy bugs, because the former are also covered with waxy filaments. The ladybird nymphs do grow larger than the mealy bugs and when disturbed move off at quite a speed. They seek out various hiding places, such as dead leaves, to pupate and you should take care not to destroy them by mistake.

When mealy bugs are in short supply, the ladybirds will eat other prey, such as scale insects. Their activity is influenced by temperature, and both adults and nymphs show little inclination to do anything below about 16°C (61°F). A tiny parasitoid chalcid wasp called *Leptomastix dactylopii* is sometimes used with the ladybirds to control mealy bugs. The wasp lays its ova inside the larger mealy bugs, where they eat the contents and then pupate in the mummified skin.

Red spider mites

Although they are called red spider mites, the red colour is shown only by the inactive hibernating form and the butterfly breeder will soon discover that this pest is in fact green, with two darker spots on the body. The mites are very small and it requires good eyesight to see them unless you resort to a magnifying glass. What can be seen more easily are some fine silky threads, often on the leaves or the leaf joints, and a deterioration of the leaves, which often become mottled. High temperatures and dry conditions speed the life-cycle, which can be very rapid. A single female can lay over 100 ova and the nymphs may reach maturity in as little as a week. An infestation can be confirmed by using the sticky tape method and seeing the eight-legged mites under a low-power

Mottled leaves, as on this Passiflora x caerulearacemosa, *can indicate the presence of red spider mites.*

microscope. Some control is obtained by keeping a high humidity around the plants, but this merely slows the mites' development. The biological control agent against red spider mite is itself a mite, this time an orange-red one. It has the Latin name *Phytoseiulus persimilis* and is just a little larger than its prey and so more readily visible. It moves much faster than its prey and eats all stages of the pest. Low humidity and temperatures above 30°C (86°F) are bad for this control agent.

Scale insects

There are many species of scale insect and they are generally divided into the so-called soft- and hard-scale types. They can be found on a wide range of plants, but are particularly common on citrus leaves. They are usually brownish in colour and can be see as small, domed scales pressed close to the midribs of the leaves.

Scale insects suck the sap from the vascular tissue and can move around from one place to another, although they are rarely seen moving. Direct damage may appear slight at the site of the scale, but they excrete honeydew and where this sticks to the leaves a thick coating of black fungal growth develops which both reduces the plant's photosynthetic efficiency and looks very unsightly.

For small outbreaks, use a paint brush and some methylated spirits or dilute washing-up liquid. You can use your fingernail or a soft sponge to remove both scale and the offensive fungal growth.

If there are already *Cryptolaemus* species present, and not an excessive number of mealy bugs, some biological control will be achieved. The specific control agent available for scale insects is the parasitoid *Metaphycus helvolus*. This is a very tiny insect which attacks the nymphs of soft-scale types only, and control will vary with the species of scale that is present. When seen under the lens, the females are yellow and the males black, but it is doubtful that you will see them on the plants even when you know that they are there. Apart from the scales killed by the nymphs developing in them, many more scales are killed by feeding adults.

Thrips

Although more than one species of thrip may be found in the greenhouse, they are not easy to distinguish from one another. The adult insect is

There are many species of scale insect. Those found on citrus leaves are usually paler and less domed than those found on woody stems.

very small and has a blackish, elongated body. The wings are small and feathery, and not membranous as are most insects' wings. When disturbed, they appear to jump off the leaves and are easily carried from one place to another. They are frequently first introduced inside flowers, where they may not be noticed. The ova are laid just under the surface of leaves and develop into nymphs which are at first colourless and then become yellowish as they grow larger. The nymphs are generally found on the underside of leaves.

An infestation of thrips can do considerable damage to sensitive plants if it is allowed to build up, which it can do quite quickly. Leaves become covered with silvery flecks and eventually shrivel up and die. When the nymphs reach full size, they pupate and the pupae fall to the ground, where the adults emerge. Thrips are seriously dangerous pests in a butterfly greenhouse because they can

The leaves of Asclepias curassavica *are easily damaged by thrips and whitefly but can be washed gently with soapy water.*

do considerable damage to *Passiflora* species and are difficult to control without pesticides.

It is possible to wash the leaves of some plants, such as *Asclepias* species, to remove infestations, but this treatment is not safe for many plants. The biological control agent for thrips is an extremely small predatory mite called *Amblyseius cucumeris*. The main problem with it is that it does not readily establish itself. It is usually supplied as a living culture on flakes of bran where it has been bred on an entirely different prey. Because they feed only on the young stages of thrips, they will, in any case, take a long time to control a serious outbreak because the adult thrips will continue to breed.

Whiteflies

Whiteflies are a common pest on greenhouse plants and need little description. The adults are clearly visible, despite their small size, because they are coated with a white waxy material and fly up in clouds when disturbed. The adults lay small groups of ova that hatch into a mobile stage that actively seeks out the veins of a leaf. They then become attached feeding 'scales' that grow and produce a sticky honeydew that encourages secondary mould growth. The nymphs pupate on

the leaves and the emerging adults move off to congregate on the young leaves of plants that are attractive to them, such as species in the genera *Asclepias* and *Lantana*.

The biological control agent for whitefly is one of the most effective available: a tiny wasp called *Encarsia formosa*. The females lay their ova in the whitefly scales, within which the larvae develop, at the same time turning the scale black. After pupation inside the scale, the adult wasp emerges through a tiny hole cut in the scale. This gives some indication of the size of the adults, which are otherwise rarely seen. The success of the control can be easily assessed by counting the number of black scales present. The control agent is supplied in the form of these black scales, often on pieces of leaf. These are distributed around the greenhouse on infested plants to allow the wasps to emerge and then find the whitefly scales. Unfortunately, the control agent does not always establish itself well on some species of plant and is rather slow to control a serious infestation of

The black 'scales' of the whitefly control agent Encarsia formosa *and the white hairy spots of an additional control, a fungal species of the genus* Verticillium.

whitefly. The tiny, metallic black, predatory beetles of the genus *Delphastus* are also available and these are supplied in the adult form. They are very helpful in controlling extensive whitefly infestations and are vigorous fliers.

Vine weevils

An adult weevil is easily recognized because its head is elongated into a pointed 'snout'. The vine weevil is about 10mm (3/8in) long and a brownish-black colour. It feeds on the leaves of plants, biting out small pieces. It has become a serious pest of potted plants because the larvae – which are whitish, legless grubs – eat the roots and can kill a plant. Only when you dig it up will the damage, and perhaps the grubs, be seen.

It is difficult to kill the underground stage, so some compost suppliers are putting insecticides into their products. You should try to avoid such poisoned composts and repot any new plants that you suspect might be growing in them.

Watch out for the adult vine weevils in the greenhouse and remove them. There is also a biological control available. This consists of a very tiny nematode worm that is a parasitoid of the vine weevil grubs. The nematodes are usually supplied in a form that has to be mixed with water and poured on to the soil. They find the vine weevil grubs and get inside them. More nematodes are liberated after the grubs have been killed, but they will, of course, not be able to move from one pot to another.

Other pests

Many other pests find their way into the tropical greenhouse. Millipedes and woodlice may accumulate where there are damp areas and can damage growing plants. They are best removed by hand, after you've lured them under a damp brick or piece of wood.

Slugs like similar conditions and are also a nuisance. You can pick them up by hand, lure them into covered slug traps baited with stale beer, or put down 'slug granules' (usually containing a toxic substance such as metaldehyde). Butterflies do not usually visit such bait, but it's best to cover it so that the only access is from the sides. Earwigs damage plants and may also take butterfly ova and young larvae. They can be trapped in inverted plastic cups filled with moss or straw and put on the tops of sticks. Each day, take the cups outside and dispose of the contents, refill and replace.

Diseases

A well-controlled tropical greenhouse should not have too many problems with diseases. Regular removal of old and dying leaves should help to prevent the fungi that are always present on such material from invading the living plants. Not all fungi can spread like this; those that can are known as facultative pathogens. Cold, damp conditions and weak plant growth due to nutrient deficiencies, low temperatures, or shortage of light, will encourage such attacks.

The obligate fungal pathogens, which only occur in living plants, are unlikely to develop into serious outbreaks. Something that does need to be considered, however, is the possibility of virus diseases. Because some sap-sucking insects are likely to be present, they may transfer viruses from one species of plant to another. In one species of plant, the virus may be without symptoms, but in another it may cause severe stunting. Other symptoms may be yellowing of the leaves, but it is not easy to distinguish this from yellowing due to other causes, such as over-watering, or alkaline tap water, or natural ageing processes.

It is also possible to confuse symptoms of nutrient deficiency with virus symptoms, so one of the important aspects of growing the plants is to ensure that they are properly supplied with all the necessary major and minor nutrients, but not so much of any one that it will promote a deficiency of another. With a little experience, the butterfly breeder will become adept at diagnosis. Whatever the cause, it is always safest to remove dead and sickly plants from the tropical greenhouse.

The black 'sooty mould' that grows on the honeydew (slightly modified plant sap) excreted by whiteflies and some other sap-feeding pests, grows on the surface of the leaves below the pest. It significantly reduces the light reaching the leaves and should be washed off if at all possible. It is always desirable to keep mould growth of any kind to an absolute minimum because spores circulating in the air may cause respiratory problems in some people. We do not recommend the use of fungicides, because their toxicity to butterflies, at any stage of the life-cycle, is largely unknown, even by the manufacturers.

7 How butterflies live

This front view of Papilio rumanzovia *clearly shows the main features of the head region.*

Butterflies have been around on the Earth for a very long time and probably evolved as a distinct type of insect at the same time that flowering plants were diversifying. This would place their origins sometime around the middle to the end of the Mesozoic period, also known as the Age of the Dinosaurs. Fossil butterflies have been found in the Florissant shales of Colorado, estimated to be 35 million years old. This is really quite surprising, because they seem so fragile and certainly disappear quite rapidly when they die and fall to the ground.

Butterflies are classified as belonging to the animal phylum Arthropoda and show the characteristics of having jointed limbs and a hard external covering rather than an internal skeleton. The term 'hard' may seem a little strange when applied to a soft larvae, but that is only the beginning of the problems that arise when we start to consider the position of butterflies in the great web of life. Butterflies are separated from many of the other arthropods by being members of the class Insecta. Actually there are more insect species than any other class of animals; about 75% of all species of animals are insects. Insects all have various features in common, the six legs being perhaps the most widely known. But simple observation shows that butterfly larvae have more than six legs, so we have to understand that there are 'true' legs and other legs! Many butterflies appear to have only four legs because one pair of legs is often much reduced in size and not used for standing on.

The life-cycle

All butterflies have what is known as a 'complete' life-cycle. The adult female, after pairing with a male, lays ova (a single one is an ovum). These hatch into larvae which feed and grow larger. They moult their skin a number of times, going through stages of growth called instars. When fully grown, a larva seeks a suitable spot in which to pupate, usually attaching itself to a support with silk.

When the final larval skin is shed, a soft pupa is revealed which normally has little in common with the shape of the original larva. The pupal skin hardens and the process known as metamorphosis takes place. The body is reassembled into that of the adult butterfly. This may take place over a period of a few days or weeks or may be delayed by many months during a 'resting' period called a diapause. Most tropical butterflies do not diapause and a new generation of adults can be present at the same time as its parents, if the adults are long-lived.

It would not be of any great help in the present book to attempt to describe all the different types of ova, all the various larvae and pupae, or all the different types of adult, or imago, butterflies that can be found. Some have been well researched and described, drawn and photographed. Others are either not well known or the information is not readily available. As for habits, foodplants and general biology, this information is even harder to find. If possible, you should keep records, drawings and photographs when you breed your own tropical butterflies. What you find out could well be unknown. When recording foodplants, please remember that it is important to record the exact species of plant, just as it is important to know the actual species of butterfly that you are breeding.

Evolution at work

The selective forces of evolution have resulted in butterflies as we see them today. Those forces act differently on the male and female, and in some cases this can lead to them being different in appearance and habits. Males must find a mate and so they are often very visible as they fly about. They may even be aggressively territorial, guarding a favoured spot and chasing off other males.

Females must survive for long enough after mating to lay their ova. This may have resulted in the selection of less active females that have a tendency to hide in the vegetation. It is obvious that butterflies such as the heliconids, which develop their ova and lay them a few at a time over many weeks, must live longer than those that lay a lot of ova in a short time.

A mating pair of Parides iphidamus. *The male is hanging below the female.*

Some male butterflies, such as *Parides* species, attach a 'mating plug' (sphragis in entomological language) to the female. This covers her genital pore and prevents subsequent males from mating with her. In some butterflies, such as the papilios, the males can be easily distinguished from the females by the presence of claspers (valvae) at the end of the abdomen, which they use to grip the female during mating. Males may also have special (androconial) patches, tufts or folds on the wings and even erectable hair pencils (more brushes than pencils) which release pheromones or 'sex dust'.

Some females produce biologically active volatile substances that attract males; those produced by mated females may even be anti-aphrodisiacs. The sex life of butterflies is very complicated – just like that of humans!

Butterfly bodies

The external structure of an adult butterfly is easy to see and needs little description. The body is divided into three regions. The head carries two elongated antennae (feelers) that often end in an expanded club region. They detect chemical stimuli important in finding mates, adult food and plants suitable for oviposition. The basal parts of the antennae also play a role in balance during flight.

Although the eyes are not thought to focus clearly, they are very sensitive to light and movement. Their sensitivity to light is not the same as ours and they can see ultraviolet light. The eyes are a major feature of the head and are called compound, because they are made up of many separate units called ommatidia (a single one is an ommatidium). Actually, there is one very simple eye, called an occellus, above each compound eye, but these are not thought to play any important role in adult vision. Usually the eyes of the males are larger than those of the females but this is not obvious.

The mouthparts of the adult are modified into a hollow tube, actually made up of two halves which are joined together all the way along by tiny spines. Occasionally the two halves can be seen separately as the adult emerges from its pupa. The proboscis, as this tube is known, is used to suck up liquids. It can be coiled and uncoiled by changes in blood pressure. Between, but below, the eyes are two palpi that vary greatly in shape and size, being especially large in butterflies that feed on rotting fruit. They may be used to wipe particles from the surface of the eyes.

The second section of the body is the thorax. This has six legs although the front pair may be very much reduced in size and not used for standing. In some butterflies, the size of this front pair differs between the males and the females. Legs are not just used for standing on; they are important sensory structures conveying information about the chemical nature of the surface that the butterfly alighted on.

There are two pairs of wings attached to the thorax. They are membranous and supported by many obvious veins. Each vein has a special name and/or number and the exact way in which the veins are arranged is important in the classification of butterflies. When describing the patterns and shapes of butterfly wings, a number of terms are used which refer to distinct areas of the wings. In butterflies, the front pair of wings are not coupled to the hind pair, but the wings do function together as a complex unit that allows great aerial agility.

In most species of butterfly, the wings are covered with scales, although some species have very few, for example the various glasswings (ithomiids). The scales are quite complex and vary in shape and size. Some are coloured by pigments, while others have very fine ridges that can diffract light. This gives them the appearance of pigments by scattering particular wavelengths of the light that is falling on them. The patterns found on the wings are truly remarkable and the exact way in which the complexity is controlled at the genetic and developmental level is not understood. Evolutionary selection has resulted in undersides that differ from upper surfaces, and males that are different from females.

The third section of the adult body is the abdomen. This contains the major part of the digestive system and the reproductive organs. There are 10 segments to the abdomen of which the last two or three are modified into the genitalia. While the head and thorax are not capable of any significant change in size, the abdomen can stretch when the digestive system is full of liquid. A butterfly that is feeding well will be much heavier than one that is short of water and nutrients. If the abdomen is soft and shrunken, then it probably needs to feed immediately.

Ova

Ova vary in shape between the different families (or subfamilies); some are almost spherical and smooth, others domed, elongated or pointed. Often, there are complex sculptural patterns on the surface. All ova have a small depression on the 'top' which is called the micropyle. This is where the sperm enters the ovum during fertilization. It happens just before the ova are laid and not when mating occurs. The micropyle also acts as a place where water vaporization and gaseous exchange can take place.

The number of ova laid by a single female varies considerably depending on the species and, of course, on whether she lives long enough to lay her full potential. A range of around 25 to 200 is generally quoted, although some species may exceed this. An average of 100 is probably a reasonable estimate.

Where the ova are laid (the oviposition site) depends on the species. Many species lay their ova on the underside of young, but expanded, leaves. Others prefer to concentrate on the growing tips of shoots. A few lay on stems or even old, dead parts of the plants, such as the dried up tendrils favoured by the heliconid *Dryas julia*. Others may lay near, but not actually on, a larval foodplant.

The number of ova laid in each batch can vary with the species: it may be a single ovum, a few or dozens. If it is a large batch, there is usually some relatively regular pattern in the arrangement. Regardless of the number of ova in a batch, most females prefer to lay away from ova laid by another butterfly.

The selection of the site is undoubtedly complex and probably depends on the shape and size of the plant and its leaves, its texture – smooth or hairy – colour and biochemical composition. Genetic factors may play a part, in that different strains within a single butterfly

The colour of these ova of Dione juno *is due to the contents, not the shell.*

species may prefer particular foodplants. Also, the selection of oviposition site may be determined by the species of plant used by the earlier stages of the life-cycle.

The colour of ova depends almost entirely on the contents because the outer shell, the chorion, is translucent. When first laid, the colour can range from white, through yellows to greens, browns and reds. As a larva develops inside the ovum, the colour may change, usually darkening. Some butterflies, such as the coontie hairstreak (*Eumaeus atala*), attach hairs to the surface of the ova as they are laid. It has been suggested that this may camouflage the ova or deter parasitoids and predators. Most ova are coated with a sticky material before they are laid. This hardens later, as does the chorion. At first there are no structures visible in the ovum, but the larval body gradually takes shape and can be seen inside just before it emerges.

Larval life

The first thing a larva does is to eat the chorion. If the ova are in a batch, the first larvae may even eat some of the other ova before they have had time to hatch. The larvae are eating machines, consisting of a hardened head capsule with prominent, strong mandibles, plus various other mouthparts, followed by a soft, rather stretchy body. The head capsule also carries, on each side, a set of very small eyes called stemmata (singular is stemma). These are sometimes called ocelli, but this is not the strictly accurate term for them. Their vision is not thought to be very good, but is possibly improved by the side-to-side head movements that the larvae often make. The head also bears two short antennae.

Apart from the head, there are usually 13 segments to the larval body. The first three are considered to be equivalent to the thorax of the adult and each has a pair of true, jointed legs. The remaining 10 segments are considered to be equivalent to the abdomen of the adult and the third, fourth, fifth, sixth and tenth each have a pair of prolegs (or false legs) that are fleshy extensions of the body armed with tiny hooks (crochets) at the ends. They are important for walking and the last pair, in particular, are important during skin changes and pupation as an anchoring point. On some segments, a pore (spiracle) is visible on each side, through which the larva breathes. These are connected to an internal complex of breathing tubes (tracheae).

As the larva grows, its skin stretches, but at various intervals the old outer skin is shed and replaced by a new one which has formed inside. During this time the larva does not feed, may move off the food plant, and then remain immobile, often looking in a very poorly state for many hours. The number of moults varies from four to seven according to the species, but the exact number can also be influenced by nutritional and environmental conditions.

The actual size, colour, shape and appearance of the larvae vary enormously and some species can be identified from the larvae alone. Some bear a complex array of spines and/or fleshy projections and it is remarkable how such species are able to shed one skin and replace it with another that is just as complex. Actually, the different stages (instars) of a larva may vary a great deal in appearance. In some species, evolutionary selection obviously acts differently as the larva progresses through the instars.

Pupation

When the larva has reached full size, it stops feeding and seeks a site for pupation. It may excrete a substantial amount of liquid and shrink considerably in size. It is then called a prepupa. Nearly all pupae are cryptically coloured and often oddly shaped. The pupal stage is relatively immobile –

*This heliconid larva (*Heliconius charitonius*) shows many of the features of a typical butterfly larva.*

Pupa of various species of tropical butterfly, showing just a few of the multitude of types, here ready for placing in a netted chamber for emergence.

although some wriggle quite actively – and is very vulnerable to predation because it is a very rich source of nutrients. Pupae vary in shape considerably, and it is sometimes possible to identify the genus or even the species from the pupa alone.

Once the prepupa has selected a suitable spot, it spins a silk pad and uses this to attach the tip of its abdomen to the chosen site. In some genera, the prepupa spins a silk pad on each side of the middle of the body and a silk girdle between the pads going around the body. The tip of the abdomen attaches itself to the terminal silk pad and the outer skin of the prepupa then splits, from the head end backwards, to reveal the soft pupal skin inside. The shape of the pupa usually bears very little resemblance to the shape of the prepupal stage.

The abdominal tip of the pupa has a set of hooks (called the cremaster) which by active wriggling it is able to extract from the old prepupal skin and attach to the silk pad. The

pupa then becomes quiescent while its skin hardens. The whole process of pupation usually takes several hours, or even days, before the pupal skin is really protective, although the actual sloughing off of the prepupal skin only takes a very short time. A soft pupa is very delicate and can be damaged easily, allowing the living contents to leak out, with fatal results.

Although the pupa is often described as a resting stage, it is actually a period of intense and complicated biochemical changes. The entire contents of the pupa are reassembled into the structure of the adult butterfly. This process of metamorphosis is still very poorly understood. In some species there is a genuine diapause at the pupal stage, but most tropical butterflies have no diapause. A day or so before the adult butterfly emerges (called eclosion), the pattern of the wings can often be seen through the pupal skin. After the pupal skin has split, the adult must get out of it very quickly to avoid becoming stuck inside it.

Some stages in the eclosion and wing expansion of the papilionid Graphium agamemnon. *The whole process takes only a matter of minutes.*

Even a part of the skin stuck on to the adult may prevent its wings from expanding normally.

The wings expand as blood is pumped into the veins that support them. This process may last only a matter of minutes and the newly emerged adult must be in a position where the wings cannot snag on anything. Once the wings have expanded and dried, nothing can be done to correct defects. If the butterfly falls off the pupal shell, or a nearby support, it is likely to be permanently crippled. Some butterflies appear to have two of their legs stuck to the pupal case as an insurance against this. When they have expanded their wings and dried off, which may take many hours, they then pull away from the pupal shell. Adults may not become fully active for some days after emergence. During this time they generally prefer to rest in a shady spot. They like to hang upside-down from a secure horizontal stem, obscured from view by the leaves above. It is best to put them in a good spot yourself, because if allowed to fly off, they often go down to the ground or start climbing up stems.

The American Papilio cresphontes *(the giant swallowtail) freshly emerged and drying its wings.*

8　Feeding and breeding

Feeding

The structure of a butterfly's mouthparts, modified as they are into a fine tube, means that it can only take in food in the form of a liquid or very fine suspension. Many species are attracted to flowers but there are some which never visit flowers; they feed instead from rotting fruit and the strong sap oozing from plants. A few do both and many tropical butterflies visit things that we would find much less desirable, such as urine and dung. These are sources of nutrients. Many tropical butterflies also use their proboscis to take up biochemicals, from plant surfaces and juices, that are the precursors of their defence and pheromone substances so essential for a successful life.

Nectar

Butterflies visit flowers for the nectar. This is high in sugars that provide instant energy for flight. Nectar varies in composition depending on the species, but most contain sugars of a low molecular weight, such as glucose, fructose and sucrose. Butterflies are generally considered to require rather weak nectars, in the range of 15 to 25% sugar, rather than the stronger nectars produced by flowers adapted to pollination by 'high energy demand species' such as hummingbirds.

Pollen

Flowers that are adapted to butterfly pollination tend to have rather more amino acids (a source of nitrogenous nutrients) in them, although these substances are always at low levels in any nectar. Although pollen cannot be directly eaten by butterflies, it is well known that many heliconid butterflies

Zebra and postman heliconids feeding from orange skins after most of the juice has been squeezed out for human consumption.

actively collect pollen on the outer surface of their proboscis. This is then manipulated with the tip of the proboscis which exudes a liquid. Nitrogenous substances leach out of the pollen grains and the enriched liquid is then reabsorbed by the proboscis. Females are said to collect greater pollen loads than males and it has been shown that the number of ova laid increases many times when pollen is available.

Sugar water

Breeders of tropical butterflies normally provide additional supplies of sugar water. It is put into a shallow tray that contains a plastic pot scourer or sponge, so that the butterflies can stand on this while sucking up the sugar water. Some breeders prefer to use honey, others pure sugars, all at a concentration of 10 to 20% (weight to volume of clean water).

Due to evaporation, the sugar concentration will rise and although butterflies are quite able to take up solutions of 40%, such high initial strengths are not recommended. Of the sugars, it is probably best to use fructose (fruit sugar as it is called commercially), because this is sweeter and there is no danger of it crystallizing inside the butterfly. Crystallization has been shown to occur sometimes with ordinary table sugar (sucrose) and it can result in the death of the butterfly. Glucose is intermediate in this respect. A sugar solution in the greenhouse is soon invaded by bacteria and fungi and needs to be replaced frequently. It is best to keep stock sugar solutions in a refrigerator and to make them up with boiling water to reduce initial microbial contamination.

The colour of the pads used in the trays may influence the visits by the butterflies and most breeders use reds and blues. The butterflies soon learn where these trays are placed. Many individual recipes can be created for more complex feeding mixtures and this is a useful subject for experiments. You could also put out small trays of dry, crushed pollen; these are visited by heliconids and others, such as the giant owls. Pollen is subject to much more rapid microbial attack than sugar water and needs to be replaced frequently. You should only put out small

Heliconius melpomene *at the flowers of* Asclepias curasavica *with a pollen load on its proboscis.*

Papilio demoleus *swallowtails feeding at sugar water pads.*

quantities, because it is expensive, and because it can be quite difficult to find a supplier of pure, untreated, pollen.

Fruit

Some butterflies, such as the brassolids and morphos, only visit fruit and it is necessary to provide them with trays of ripe and over-ripe samples, otherwise their life-span and reproductive capacity will be very much reduced. Most fruits soften naturally when over-ripe, but you may need to split tough skins to provide access to the pulp. You can use the skins from fruit that you have already eaten, but this usually has only a small amount of flesh adhering to it and, even more

Adults of Greta oto *attracted to a dead member of the same species.*

importantly, tropical fruit may have been exposed to high concentrations of pesticides, either before or after harvest, to prolong storage life. These may be harmful and cannot easily be removed by washing; nor can you determine their presence. Fruit grown under the organic (no pesticide) system is excellent, but do be sure that the grower has not used any bacterial spray to control caterpillars. It is better to use the whole inside of the fruit. Bananas and mangoes are particularly attractive to brassolids, but melons, oranges, apples and many other fruits can be used.

Although a little yeasty fermentation does not appear to cause any problems, it is best to change the fruit when mould growth covers the surface and before spores are liberated into the closed atmosphere of the heated greenhouse. You can also make up mixtures of pulped fruit, sugar water and other substances, such as beer. Trays with these foods in them should not be placed on the ground, because they will attract less desirable insects. You can hang them up, from the roof or place them on stands at lower levels. If ants are a problem, the food trays should be placed on a low support, such as a plastic lid from a jar in the centre of a dish of water which will act as a moat.

Water

Without water, adults will dry up and die, so they often suck up moisture from the surface of plants or damp ground. This liquid will contain all sorts of other substances, such as mineral salts and complex organic substances. These may be important nutrients or otherwise beneficial substances for the butterfly. Large congregations of butterflies are often seen on damp mud patches or at sap oozing from damaged plants. It has been shown that sodium is an important element to butterflies and this is probably one of the main reasons why they visit mud patches. Even if the ground is dry, butterflies may be attracted to it. They probably exude a saliva that is then sucked up again once salts have dissolved into it. In the greenhouse, a tray containing dilute sea salt solution may prove useful. We do not recommend pouring salt solution directly on to sand or soil, because this frequently encourages bacteria that produce an unpleasant smell, at least it is to humans. In *Butterflies of the World*, Rod and Ken Preston-Mafham describe how tropical butterflies congregated on a spot where clothes had been washed. Some washing powders contain high concentrations of sodium and phosphates and these may have remained in the soil after the more toxic ingredients had been washed away. It is not stated whether a washing soap or powder had been used, but if not what was attracting the butterflies may have had a human origin. Fresh washing powders and liquids are, of course, toxic. It appears that male butterflies are more likely to visit mud patches than females and in a few species the females actually obtain additional sodium from the males during mating.

The need for nitrogen

The females generally require more nitrogenous substances than the males due to ova production. In their search for nitrogenous compounds, adult butterflies are attracted to many rather unpleasant things. Dead animals, urine, both animal and human, and dung, particularly that from carnivorous animals, are all feasts to many tropical butterflies. This may be related to the poor availability of other sources of nitrogen in tropical regions. You are unlikely to welcome these substances in your tropical greenhouse, but the need for nitrogen should not be ignored and more acceptable sources may prove useful for some species.

Breeding

Adult butterflies have only one real purpose in life and that is to stay alive long enough to find a mate, pair up and leave as many offspring as possible. To achieve this, males and females must meet. It used to be thought that females chose the most flamboyant males and that this is the reason why butterflies are often so colourful and why males are sometimes more brightly coloured than females. Much of this theory was transferred to butterflies from observations on birds and was not based on direct observations. It was taken to be fact even by Darwin in his discussions of sexual selection.

Finding each other

Although there have not been very many proper experiments, we do now know that the situation is much more complex than that. Many of the bright colour patterns on butterflies are in fact warning colorations, while some of the undoubted sex recognition patterns are not visible to humans because they rely upon the ultraviolet vision of the butterflies. In fact, it is often the males that seek out the females and frequently it is chemical rather than visual signals that are important, particularly in the case of danaids, heliconids and ithomiids. That this should be so seems rather obvious when we remember that mimicry between different species and multiple colour and pattern forms within a single species are very common among tropical butterflies. This fact was, of course, well known to Darwin's contemporary Henry Walter Bates who gave his name to Batesian mimicry.

Territorial males

In most species of butterflies there is competition between the males to mate with the females and males may establish territories or patrol certain places, chasing off other males that stray into their space. Sometimes the territories may only be held

for a few hours and it appears that, because of their poor vision, butterflies will fly to investigate almost any appropriate moving object in their space. In the absence of females, invading males generally fly away when approached. In some species, visual clues are certainly important in recognizing whether a flying butterfly is male or female even if humans cannot see the difference.

Pheromones

Pheromones are also important. Female butterflies generally mate very soon after they have emerged, whereas males may take several days before they are ready to mate. During this time they may be accumulating precursors of their pheromones from plants, as is the case of most danaids. In some species, the female produces pheromones

Adults of Greta oto *collecting precursors of pheromones from a bunch of dried* Senecio vulgaris.

that attract males. One of the best-known examples is the heliconid *Heliconius charitonius* where even the pre-emergence female pupa will attract males eager to mate at the earliest opportunity with the virgin female.

Courtship rituals

Butterfly courtship rituals are often very elaborate and in some species quite a large flight area may be necessary. Although some females may mate more than once, it is often found that a female that has already paired will not respond to the advances of subsequent males. She will either fly away, or land and place her wings or abdomen in such a position that the male cannot reach the tip of it.

The courtship flights of giant owl butterflies are vigorous and require a reasonable space.

A female Heliconius hecale *with the tip of the abdomen raised to deter the sexual advance of males.*

If the male's advances are accepted initially it is found that, in the many species that have androconial scales or hair pencils, the male must transfer some of these scales, the so-called 'love dust', to the female's antennae before the next stage can take place. Sometimes this occurs during flight. In other species, the female lands and the male hovers above her before landing alongside and placing the tip of his abdomen close enough to hers for him to grasp her with his anal claspers. Mating then occurs. In some species, such as all papilionids, the anal claspers are very obvious.

Mating

The coupling is quite strong and the pair can fly, one with wings beating and the other hanging down as an inert passenger. This will take them to a selected sheltered spot where the pair may remain together for anything from minutes to hours. During this time, the butterflies are very vulnerable to predation and the patterns on the underside of the wings are of the utmost importance for camouflage or warning. In some species, the male transfers a 'mating plug' to prevent further matings as well as the spermatophore which contains sufficient sperm to fertilize all the ova that the female either already has or will produce during her life-time. In others, the female may produce anti-aphrodisiac pheromones after she has mated.

In most butterflies, there is little that can be done to encourage mating other than providing appropriate conditions in terms of heat, light and humidity and any plants necessary for pheromone production. Many butterflies appear to mate only at certain times of the day and this is likely to be at a different time from feeding activity. The ithomiid, *Mechanitis isthmia*, for example, pairs between 10a.m. and 1p.m., while *Danaus chrysippus* prefers the late afternoon. Obviously, courtship flights require a lot of energy and it is essential to have a good supply of nectar plants, with supplementary sugar water if necessary, to encourage pairing. A daylength of less than 12 hours is unlikely to promote courtship, nor is a temperature of less than 25°C (77°F). It is sometimes found that a mating pair has not separated even after 24 hours. Although this may occur naturally, it may be because the pair has been resting in an atmosphere that is too dry and has become stuck together. In this circumstance it is worth applying a little warm water, using a fine paint-brush, to the joined tips of their abdomens.

Assisted pairing

With most butterflies, it is not possible to assist the mating process by direct human intervention. With some of the larger butterflies, particularly the papilionids, it is possible to assist nature by 'hand pairing'. In general, the female should be freshly emerged and the male a few days old. There are several descriptions of the process, which differ in detail, but practical experience is really the only guide to this very delicate process. Basically, you should take the male and female in separate hands, holding them by the wings with the tips of their abdomens facing each other. The claspers of the male must be open and if this is not the case, they can be encouraged by a little very gentle pressure on the male's abdomen. Then, bring the genitalia into close contact and, with luck, the male claspers will grasp the female and after a minute or so the pair can be placed in a suitable shady spot.

If you don't obtain a firm coupling after two or three attempts, it is unlikely that coupling will occur and the attempts should stop and the butterflies released to feed and fly. The process requires a detailed knowledge of butterfly sexual

Two different patterns of Heliconius melpomene *in a pairing, presumably using scent rather than vision to find each other. However, the warning coloration of the underside is still obvious.*

anatomy and is only to be recommended when the provision of a proper environment has not proved sufficient in itself to promote natural pairing.

It should be noted that there are a very few species, of which the famous monarch (*Danaus plexippus*) is the classic example, where there is no attempt by the male at a complicated courtship. In this species, which is a robust and strong flier, the male virtually knocks the female to the ground and then mates with her. Many breeders find that the monarch does not mix easily with other butterflies because it is liable to knock them to the ground too, causing injury or even death.

9   The young ones

Warning coloration on a larva of Junonia octavia, *feeding on a variegated coleus cultivar.*

available to breeders is the tiny *Talicada nyseus* which feeds inside some species of *Kalanchoe* and *Bryophyllum*.

Larvae which feed on leaves are subject to two important dangers. One is desiccation, which they overcome by feeding at night and resting during the day on the underside of leaves rather than the top. These two strategies also provide protection against the second danger: being eaten. This may also be avoided by disguise, looking, for example, like a bird dropping. This is a tactic employed by many citrus-feeding papilionids. Warning coloration, indicating that the larva is unpalatable, and irritant hairs, are more positive forms of defence against predation.

Larval food

The majority of butterfly larvae feed on the leaves of flowering plants (angiosperms); only a few feed on the leaves of the other group of seed plants, the gymnosperms, which includes the conifers and cycads. Ferns and other 'lower' types of plant life are rarely used as foodplants.

Although the nutritional value of leaves is not considered to be very high, butterflies and moths are more efficient at converting leaves into insect body weight than most other insects. Very few butterfly larvae burrow into plants (known as endofeeders). One of the few that is sometimes

Temperature

Regardless of the species of foodplant, all larvae have a particular temperature range over which they are active and this may differ from one species to another.

For most tropical butterflies, little is known about the lowest temperature for feeding, or the highest temperature they will survive. The minimum for feeding is generally well above that which would cause death. Obviously, death due to desiccation can occur, even when the temperature itself is not a danger. Between these two extremes, feeding takes place, but there will be an optimum

*The tiny red pierrot (*Talicada nyseus*) has larvae small enough to feed hidden inside plant tissues.*

The young larvae of citrus-feeding swallowtails look like bird-droppings; the older ones look quite different.

temperature at which growth takes place most efficiently and this is always nearer to the maximum than the minimum.

Between the minimum and the optimum temperatures, it is generally found that a rise in temperature of 10°C (50°F) produces a doubling of the rate of development. This relationship is embodied in the concept known as the temperature coefficient and it applies to almost all living processes (except photosynthesis in plants when there is not enough available light).

The only way that a larva can increase its own temperature is to be in the sun and some larvae appear to need sunlight, or at least quite bright light, before they will feed. At the same time, of course, the temperature of the foodplant will also rise due to its own absorption of sunlight.

What is on the menu?

Plant-feeding butterfly larvae can be divided roughly into those which will only eat one species of plant (monophagous) and those which will eat several, often botanically related, species (polyphagous). Much has been written about the possible coevolution between plants and butterflies, but this is not of any great practical significance to the breeder. What is more important is that some plants contain substances that deter feeding, while others have properties

that stimulate feeding. Only a few plant materials are neutral in this respect.

The foodplants listed in books on tropical butterflies are almost always the ones that have been recorded in the wild. For some, it has been found that they will eat others in the greenhouse. Just because ova have been laid on a particular plant, does not mean that the larvae will be able to complete their development on it. When only the genus and not the particular species of plant is given, the breeder can only try species in that genus that *are* available, starting with those from

The larvae of the giant owls are polyphagous and will eat various species of banana and many other plants.

*Larvae of the tailed jay (*Graphium agamemnon*) feed naturally on the leaves of* Annona *species, but will also feed on those of unrelated* Magnolia *species.*

*This palm has been almost overwhelmed by too large a population of larvae of the palm fly (*Elymnias hypermnestra*), but new growth is appearing.*

the country that the butterfly naturally inhabits. For polyphagous species the choice is obviously wider. It is worth remembering that plants in cultivation have often been derived from intentional or accidental crossing between separate species and also that there is often even more variation within a species of plant than there is within a species of butterfly and this can be in terms of palatability as well as appearance.

Carnivores and cannibals

Although the butterflies described later in this book all have larvae that feed on leaves, it should be remembered that there are many carnivorous butterfly larvae, particularly amongst the lycaenids, and that the breeding of these is beyond the scope of this book. Note also that most larvae eat their own egg shells and may start eating unhatched ova nearby. Some larvae are gregarious, but others are solitary and may well attack and eat nearby larvae. This is very likely if the nearby larva has just changed its skin. Some larvae will eat their own skin after it has been shed. Overcrowding and shortage of foodplant will promote cannibalism and may be a cause of losses during transport.

The best place for larvae

Female tropical butterflies usually lay their ova on or near the larval foodplant and when the larvae hatch and start feeding this is the best place to leave them. There are, however, a few reasons why this may not be possible. Firstly, there may be too many larvae for the plant to support, and you may have an additional supply elsewhere. Secondly, while you may have enough foodplant to feed all the larvae, they may be aggressive towards one

Cethosia biblis *lays its ova in batches and the larvae feed together on the leaves.*

another, either directly by being cannibalistic or indirectly by eating through stems of whole shoots, which then wilt, thereby depleting the food supply. Thirdly, it may not be possible at certain times to maintain an adequate environment in a large greenhouse. Fourthly, the larvae may wander a long way from their foodplant or into places that are unsuitable for them.

*These ova of the zebra (*Heliconius charitonius*) have been laid much closer together than normal due to a lack of other suitable sites. The larvae may need separating after they have hatched.*

Moving and housing larvae

Young larvae can be removed from a plant with a fine paint brush or on a small piece of leaf. At first they can be put into a small, clear plastic box. You can obtain suitable ones in a range of sizes and with built-in air vents. These boxes must be kept out of direct sunlight because the contents will heat up to lethal temperatures. You should examine them on a daily basis and keep them very clean.

At first, you will need to increase the humidity slightly with a small plug of damp tissue, but later you may require dry tissue to soak up excess moisture. Variations in day and night temperatures can result in dangerous condensation that may trap small larvae by capillary forces.

As the larvae grow, they will have to be transferred on to potted plants or cut shoots standing in damp florist's foam. You can use jars of water, but you will have to plug the neck firmly with cotton wool to prevent the larvae from entering them. In some cases, shoots standing in water appear to take up too much water for the larvae to cope with and this may lead to disease, as will any attempt to overcrowd the larvae. An alternative and less destructive approach (for the plants, that is) is to place the larvae on a large shoot of a growing plant, but to confine them in one place by means of a fine netted 'sleeve'. These are available in various designs and sizes.

Preventing wanderlust

When larvae reach full size, they often start to wander off the foodplant and may select quite unsuitable spots in which to pupate. These may seem right to the larvae at the time, but may be

This nearly fully grown larva of Danaus chrysippus *has moved from the leaves to a young, nutrient-rich seed pod for a final feed before pupating.*

subject to overheating as the sun moves round or be in cold spots where pupation may be delayed, and delay will increase the chances of predation at the prepupal stage. Wanderlust can be overcome with netted 'sleeves' or by placing the obviously prepupal larvae, which usually have a different appearance, into a netted pupation box where they will not be disturbed. Any pupae that are found in unsuitable spots should, of course, be removed gently and placed in the emergence box for safety.

The emergence box

An emergence box is essential for any butterfly greenhouse. It need not be large and a cube of about 30cm (12in) each way would be sufficient for most domestic greenhouses. Any pupae that are brought in from elsewhere must be placed in this box. The netting must be the finest that is available to ensure that any parasitoids that emerge from the pupae will be contained and not allowed to escape into the greenhouse. The pupae must be attached to suitable supporting sticks,

using a non-toxic glue, and the sticks elevated to leave at least one and a half times the length of one wing of the adult butterfly below it. Remember that the butterfly may be several times larger than the pupa when its wings are fully expanded.

The box should be put in a warm place, shaded from direct sun and, if the atmosphere is dry, you should spray it with clean water from time to time. You must inspect it daily and allow the emerged butterflies to fly out once their wings have fully expanded. If the wings are expanded but not yet hardened, which can take many hours in some species, you can take them out if it is absolutely necessary. Hold them gently by the wings and place them in a shaded spot for the wings to harden fully.

Emergence difficulties

From time to time an emerging butterfly may have difficulty getting out of its pupal case, particularly if it has dried slightly. You can use a pair of fine-pointed forceps and a blunt-tipped needle to remove pieces of the pupal case. Although it is difficult to determine the sex of most butterfly pupae, it is often found that the females emerge from slightly larger pupae than the males. Remember, however, that regardless of sex, the pupae and adults from larvae reared at high temperatures are normally smaller than those reared at lower ones.

After a butterfly has emerged from its pupal skin, it will usually produce a drop of coloured liquid. This contains waste substances produced during metamorphosis. This liquid should not be allowed to fall on to other pupae, because it may damage them; nor should you get it on your clothes, because it can prove impossible to remove.

With species like Heliconius melpomene *which lay over a period of many days, there will be many different larval ages present at any one time and temperature may affect them in different ways.*

The length of the life-cycle

People often ask how long it takes for a butterfly to pass from ova to adult. There is no simple answer, because it depends on the conditions. Given a greenhouse with sufficient facilities to produce constant conditions, it would be possible to breed butterflies at various temperatures and accurately measure how long was spent in the ovum, how long each instar of the larval period lasted and how long it was before the adult emerged from the pupa. Because, over an appropriate temperature range, the rate of growth is related to the temperature, it would be possible to work out how many days at a particular temperature were needed for, say, the larval stage. This quantity has been calculated for some pests and is expressed in units called 'day-degrees'.

Actually, the calculation of 'day-degrees' or similar units used by other biologists is not simple, because temperatures are never constant; they go up and down on a daily and seasonal basis, even in most tropical climates. It is true to say that we know virtually nothing about such details for even the most studied butterflies. Those who grow plants commercially in greenhouses have worked out 'blueprints' for the production of a few plant species and it would, in theory, be possible to do the same for common and rare

This prepupal stage of Papilio demoleus *has chosen an unsuitable site for pupation.*

butterflies. This would help to ensure their survival and even help to predict the effect of such dramatic events as global climate changes. The first stage must be for more people to establish living tropical greenhouses in which butterflies can be studied and expertise developed.

10 Why some butterflies die

Even when you have created a suitable environment, with healthy plants, you will still have a number of problems to overcome. All stages of the butterfly life-cycle must be protected from the predators, parasitoids and diseases which afflict them. This is quite distinct from the friends and foes of the plants discussed earlier in this book, although the basic principles mentioned at the start of that chapter are also of relevance here.

Problems with the butterflies

Many of the problems that beset butterfly livestock are the reverse of those that trouble the plants. The butterflies are what we want and the things that control their numbers are what must be eliminated. So what are the mortality factors that control butterfly numbers? Despite the great efforts being made in butterfly conservation, we have very little accurate data on this and virtually none for the majority of tropical butterflies. The first step is to identify the individual factors that might be operating. This is not too difficult. If we give them the code letter F, we can list some of them. Starting with a newly emerged female these might be:

F1   Is there a successful mating?
F2   Is there a plant present on which the ova can be laid?
F3   Will the mated female live long enough to lay her full potential of ova?
F4   Will some of the ova be eaten by predators, destroyed by parasitoids or pathogenic micro-organisms?
F5   Is there enough larval foodplant available for all the larvae that hatch?
F6   Will the larvae die before they reach the pupation stage due to parasitoids, predators

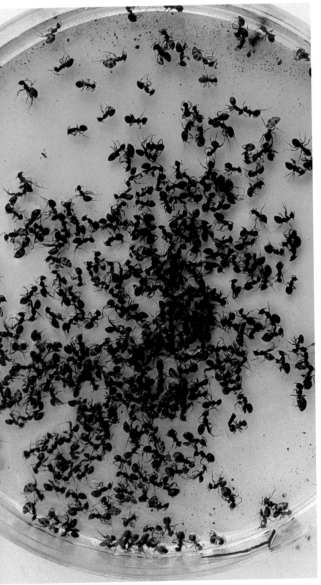

Ants can be a serious problem in a living tropical greenhouse and it can be difficult to find an effective attractant.

(small and large), or pathogenic micro-organisms?

F7 Will pupae die due to similar causes noted in F6?

F8 Will the imagos die before they have mated?

Many of these factors can be subdivided to show the precise cause of death. By using some relatively simple mathematics that have already been developed by ecologists, and after the proper quantitative observations have been made, it is possible to determine what are the 'key' factors controlling population numbers. There are also 'density dependent' factors that cause more deaths in large populations and 'regulating' factors that tend to keep populations at a steady size. The aim of the butterfly breeder is to minimize all mortality factors. A good quarantine procedure to prevent the entry of harmful organisms should go hand in hand with good plant culture techniques and a satisfactory greenhouse environment. Some of the potential problems are described below.

Spiders

Many species of spider will inevitably enter your tropical greenhouse and find the conditions very favourable for their reproduction. Ground-dwelling species will kill adult butterflies, especially when the butterflies are inactive at night or due to low temperatures at soil level. Any plant pots that you bring into the greenhouse should be inspected thoroughly for spiders or their silken egg masses. A fine spray of water will show up any webs in the corners of the greenhouse and the spiders can then be removed.

The so-called crab spiders, which do not spin significant webs but stay hidden in flowers or leaves, are a serious problem, because they will easily kill both adults and larvae. Even a very tiny spider can kill an adult butterfly many times larger than itself. The most obvious sign of a spider attack is a butterfly that is twitching uncontrollably or has folded its wings back under its body. Ordinary garden spiders and their aerial (orb) webs can be easily seen and removed. Look for signs of spider occupation behind fixtures and in any crevices.

A rare case of mistaken identity. Heliconius charitonius *has paired with* Heliconius melpomene. *No fertile ova will be produced. Factor F1.*

Heliconius charitonius *adults roost together for protection. Factor F8.*

Ants

Many tropical plants, including passion flowers, have adaptations, such as nectar glands outside of the flowers, to attract ants. Ants will carry away butterfly ova, attack and kill larvae and rapidly destroy the bodies of any butterflies they come across on the ground. Ants will soon discover the ideal environment in a tropical greenhouse and enter in their hundreds from outside nests, or worse still, set up nests inside. The first step in preventing them is to form a good seal between the greenhouse and its base, using a silicone or other mastic material to fill any cracks.

There are some commercially available baits that are attractive to ants. They consist of a slow-acting poison. The simple inorganic substance borax is a good example. It is taken back to the nest and spread to other ants there. Obviously such baits should be covered to prevent the butterflies feeding on them. Unfortunately, ants cannot be relied upon to take these baits, but after some experimentation you should be able to devise a mixture for the particular ants that are present.

Ants like a balanced diet of carbohydrate and protein, and at times they will ignore the butterflies and eat nectar from the plants. At other times they will seek out ova or larvae and carry them away. They will also kill adult butterflies and they find the abdomens of females, with their large masses of immature ova, particularly attractive. Ant nests are difficult to destroy. Boiling water with a few drops of washing-up liquid may work, but it doesn't always penetrate deeply enough to kill the queen. Obviously every effort should be made to destroy winged ants before they have a chance to spread out and start new colonies.

Any nests that you find you should dig out as completely as possible. Some ants prefer to build their nests in the soil of potted plants. If this happens you should take the plants outside and shake off the loose soil. The roots should then be immersed in water for some time to clean off any remaining soil and ants. The ants may be right inside a root ball and in small air pockets, and great care is needed if the plant is to be saved and repotted in fresh soil. Any outside nests that are near the greenhouse should also be tackled.

Other predators

Earwigs will eat butterfly ova and attack larvae and adults. Ground beetles will kill anything they come across, but hide rather obviously under pots. There are some carnivorous black slugs that attack butterflies and they may be responsible for holes in the butterflies' wings. Even if you don't see the slugs themselves, their slime trails should give them away.

Parasitoids

There are many species of flies and wasps that attack butterflies at ovum, larval and pupal stages. If the greenhouse is clean to start with and you have given sufficient time for the plants to develop, there should not be any parasitoids present when breeding commences. Provided windows and doors are protected with the finest possible netting, they should not be able to enter by that route. Therefore, the most likely way they will get in is with new livestock. It is essential, therefore that livestock is obtained from a reputable supplier and that even then it is treated as a potential source of parasitoids. One of the most serious parasitoids that can be introduced is *Pteromalus puparum*. The females lay a single ovum in a pupa before the skin has hardened and this then divides into dozens of individuals that develop inside the apparently viable pupa. These subsequently emerge through a tiny pin-hole, mate and fly off to attack further pupae. Once let out they are difficult to control.

Diseases

There are a number of bacterial and viral diseases which infect butterflies. They are most obvious when the larvae die, but they may carry over into the pupae, or even the adults, before proving lethal. It is likely that most larvae are carrying

This pupa looks normal except for the angular pin-hole exit made by Pteromalus puparum.

infectious micro-organisms, but they do not develop unless there is a significant stress from overcrowding or poor conditions. Some breeders surface sterilize ova, but this is a procedure that requires some considerable skill and should not be necessary in a well-run greenhouse. Any larvae that die should be removed as soon as possible. You should also remove the leaf they were on, because it is likely that they will have exuded liquid bearing the disease.

Larvae introduced from elsewhere may develop serious disease symptoms after being introduced into your conditions, so take care when obtaining livestock. It should be remembered that many 'organic' gardeners use a lethal preparation of bacteria to control larvae they do not want on their plants. Take care never to bring plants treated with this 'safe' insecticide into the greenhouse, because what it really amounts to is germ warfare against butterflies.

You may find that larvae obtained from other breeders rapidly die when brought into your own greenhouse. This may be due to the stress of the journey or the change in conditions or even a change in foodplant. Not all plants with the same label are exactly the same genetically. If other breeders have trouble with your own good livestock, it may also be that they have inadvertently purchased a plant containing a long-lasting systemic insecticide. This fact is not always known to the supplier of the plant because it may have been sprayed before they got it, or they may have forgotten that they have sprayed everything with some 'safe' substance.

Quails

Many butterfly houses have colonies of ground-dwelling Chinese painted quails. These birds can be very valuable, because they eat almost anything that moves on or near the ground, including ants and spiders. They can, however, develop a taste for butterflies and may even take those with warning coloration.

In a large greenhouse, quails do more good than harm, but in a small one they may be destructive. They are able to fly, but generally only do so when frightened and then they fly

Chinese painted quails will clear up pests from the ground. The ones shown here are the silver variety.

A female Chinese painted quail on her simple nest at the base of some plants.

straight up! They can be aggressive towards each other and in a small greenhouse you only need one male with one or two females.

Quails will eat small seeds and mealworms, and these you will need to supply. Their nests are usually very simple affairs, on the ground or in a box. There are many different colour forms and also much variation in the personality of individual birds, with some being more aggressive or more inclined to eat the butterfly livestock than others. It is a matter of conditions and judgement as to whether they are desirable.

Butterflies for paradise

The amount of blue on the wings of giant owl butterflies varies considerably from one species to another.

Among the insects, around 140,000 species belong to the order Lepidoptera, which includes both butterflies and moths. Most people like to think that they know the difference between butterflies, which are commonly referred to as Rhopalocera, and moths, known as Heterocera. The former are generally day-flying and have thickened ends to their antennae, while the latter are mostly night-flying and have tapered or feathery antennae. Specialists in the subject do not generally accept such divisions because there are so many exceptions. Even more controversy surrounds the

grouping together of the various species into families (which all end in the letters 'idae' and subfamilies (ending in 'inae'). Different books use different schemes, but this is not really a problem that affects the breeder.

Breeders deal with the final unit, the species. In this section we have used a simplified system of grouping the species under headings that do not strictly define taxonomic relationships.

Many butterfly species have 'common' names in English and different ones in other languages. A 'scientific' or Latin name is the same in every language and so it is used as a precise means of communicating to others the actual species that is being discussed. It is the peg on which all the known information about a species is hung and can be found by other people. It is therefore important to know it if you are breeding butterflies.

Unfortunately the names of species consist of two parts and this leads to some difficulties. The first word gives information about the relationship of a species to other species. Closely related species are put into the same genus (first word). When study shows that the relationship is not as was first thought then this word is changed, according to very precise Codes of Nomenclature. Books written at different times may have different names for the same species. To help overcome this problem many books have an index which lists separately both the first (generic) name and the second (specific) which may be less often changed but may be the same for totally unrelated species.

The Latin name by which a species is known is actually the name given to a single dead 'type' specimen which is kept in one of the great museums. New species are still being discovered and given new names, but what actually constitutes a new species is a matter of considerable debate and only really the province of the expert. Even species may be divided up into smaller subcategories, such as subspecies and forms. *Heliconius melpomene*, for example, has over 30 different patterns to the wings, which to the uninitiated look like different species. Many of these are almost exactly mimicked by patterns on the wings of a different species, *Heliconius erato*.

The following accounts of just a few species of tropical butterflies are intended only as an introduction to the subject. None of the species described is rare or endangered on a global basis, although this does not mean that they are found in large numbers everywhere in the tropics. They are all species which, from time to time, are readily available from breeders and are suitable for breeding in the type of tropical greenhouse described previously. Not all families (or subfamilies) are included. There are many books which describe some of the enormous variations in adult butterfly structure and appearance.

BRASSOLIDS

Brassolids are generally known by the name of owls, because of the very large and prominent eye-spots that are found on the underside of the hindwings, especially in the genus *Caligo*. They are all from tropical Central/South America and while some experts consider them to be a separate family, others make them only a subfamily within the large family, Nymphalidae.

There are about 80 species in the family spread over several (some say 12) genera, but all are essentially dusk and dawn fliers, although they may occasionally fly at other times. The resemblance to moths is most marked in the genus *Dynastor* which in the shape of the wing and body looks very like some silkmoths.

Some members of the *Caligo* genus are very large, with 200mm (8in) wingspans. Obviously the larvae will grow to a large size and consume a considerable amount of foodplant, which in this instance includes cultivated bananas. This has of course led to them being classified as a pest species. The genus *Brassolis* also contains large butterflies and the larvae of some are pests on coconut palms, where several hundred can be found resting in a silken 'tent' during the day. At the smaller end of the scale is the genus *Narope* with wingspans of only about 60mm (2^1/$_2$in). All genera feed on monocotyledonous plants and many have an extensive range of potential foodplants.

Giant owl (*Caligo memnon*)

Although *Caligo memnon* is not the largest of the giant owls, it is possibly the best for the beginner. The larvae of the slightly larger *Caligo eurilochus* seem to eat a great deal more foodplant than those of *C. memnon*. Also, the adults do not pair so readily in a small greenhouse. For all the *Caligo* species, a large flight area is needed, because the pre-nuptial chases are very vigorous, with frequent short rest stops, perhaps on the human observer. Despite this, the adults are quite agile and seem to avoid tall plants easily. In flight the wings make a distinct sound, even described by some as a clatter, but we liken it more to the swish of soft velvet. You should take care when leaving the greenhouse, because it is very easy to walk out of the greenhouse with one resting on your back or hair.

The underside patterning of the owls is complex, and varies between the species. The upperside of *C. memnon* has distinct broad yellowish bands on a brownish background with only a little tinging of blue-violet. The latter colour is most developed in *C. atreus*, but this species is not so easy to breed and so is not readily available.

Adult butterflies can live for many months, but they must be fed a substantial diet. They do not visit flowers and need to be provided with rotting fruit, such as bananas, oranges and mangoes. A popular recipe contains bananas mashed with a little yoghurt, fruit sugar, yeast and apple or orange juice.

The pink fruits of Musa uranoscopus *splitting open to reveal the black seeds embedded in white flesh.*

They lay their ova in small batches, not usually exceeding half a dozen, over a long period. At first the ova are white, but they turn darker, if they are fertile, after a day or two and under warm conditions will hatch in about 12 days. Although the various species of *Musa* (bananas) are the preferred larval foodplant, the larvae will take a wide variety of monocotyledonous plants, such as cannas (cultivated species and hybrids of the genus *Canna*), ginger lilies (*Hedychium* species), *Calathea* species and some others.

The larvae feed at night, when the temperature in the greenhouse must be kept high if a rapid life-cycle is required. During the day, the larvae, when young, generally line up along the underside of the midrib, on a path of silken threads. It is not wise to disturb them when small because they can become disorientated if separated from their fellows. For the first few instars the larvae are greenish, but the older instars are brown and prefer to rest on the 'stem' (actually the leaf-stalks in botanical language). The larvae have a distinct head capsule, which is crowned with horns, a few soft pseudospines along the back and a distinct forked tail. They grow to at least 10cm (4in) in length and 1cm (1/2in) in diameter and in the process will eat at least one, or more, banana leaves of a metre (39in) in length. Naturally, they prefer soft, fresh leaves rather than old, tough ones. The larval stage lasts about 45 days, or much longer if the temperature is low.

When ready to pupate, the larva shrinks by several centimetres and looks very poorly as it hangs down from the silken pad that it spins. This may be on a midrib of the foodplant, but the larva can also wander for considerable distances before pupating. The pupa is much shorter, but thicker, than the prepupal larva and female pupae are generally a little larger than those of the males. Pupation is a critical time, because the freshly formed pupa is very delicate and the slightest disturbance can cause the soft skin to burst, with fatal results. This is particularly true of the slightly larger *C. eurilochus*. Once hardened, the pupae are quite robust and it takes around three weeks for the adults to emerge, there being no diapause.

Pupae of giant owl (Caligo memnon).

DANAIDS

There are between 150 and 300 species of danaids and they are considered to be either a family of their own or a subfamily of the Nymphalidae. There are generally considered to be three groups of danaids. The first contains the genera *Ituna* and *Lycorea* and is considered to be closely related to the ithomiids. Like the latter, they are essentially Central and South American butterflies. The second group of genera contains *Danaus*, *Idea*, *Ideopsis* and *Amauris*.

In the third group (the crows) is the genus *Euploea*, which contains the greatest number of species of danaids. The life of most danaids is closely interlinked with that of certain families of plants and many require complex chemicals from the plants in order to produce pheromones essential for successful mating. Some of the chemicals which make both larvae and adults distasteful to predators come from the larval foodplants and as with all butterfly breeding, botany and entomology go hand in hand.

There are some small danaids with wingspans of about 50mm (2in), but most are in the region of 90mm (3¹/₂in) and a few are as large as 180mm (7in). The crows have a predominantly black coloration, but other species have clear warning patterns of stripes, often with bright colours. Many totally unrelated species of butterflies have developed very similar patterns and coloration as a form of protective mimicry and butterflies that look the same are not always the same species.

The ova of danaids are generally dome-shaped with distinct ribbing. They are usually laid singly, but several may be found on an individual leaf, especially if there is a shortage of foodplant. The foodplants used by the majority of species come from the families Asclepiadaceae, Apocyanaceae and Moraceae. Many species in these families are known to contain cardiac glycosides (poisons).

The larvae of danaids are usually boldly marked with bright colours and often rings or stripes. They are usually smooth, but have one or more pairs of fleshy filaments that are considered to be deterrents to predators. Species like *Danaus plexippus* have very rapid larval growth, are

Bunches of dried groundsel provide danaids with essential biochemicals.

prolific and have larvae that consume a great deal of foodplant. It is essential for breeders to have a very large supply of good plants ready. They cannot be grown from seed quickly enough to satisfy hungry larvae.

The pupae of danaids are particularly attractive. In relation to the size of the final butterfly they are relatively small and of a rounded, but somewhat elongated, shape. Many are partially, or even completely marked with gold or silver, often on a jade green background. As they hang down from their silken pads they look like jewelled, drop earrings. The pupal case is usually quite thin and so the pupae are rather delicate. The wing patterns can often be seen through the pupal case just before emergence, although some may appear almost black at that time.

There are several different colour forms of the very common butterfly Danaus chrysippus, *or plain tiger.*

Some adult danaid butterflies live a long time, particularly those that have winter roosts, such as the monarch and common crow. Daylength and temperature may play significant roles in this; it is not a true hibernation, because the adults fly and feed when conditions are favourable. This type of behaviour may not be shown in a heated and lighted greenhouse.

For the successful mating of danaids, it is normally essential to have certain species of plants present in the greenhouse in addition to the known larval foodplants. Some of these will provide nectar alone, but others are visited also for the alkaloids (poisons) they contain. It is wise to have flowering plants of *Heliotropium* and *Senecio* in the greenhouse and you could use other genera that are known to contain the essential alkaloids. You can even hang up bunches of bruised plants if there is not room to plant them. It is easier for the butterflies to obtain what they need from damaged plants.

Plain tiger (*Danaus chrysippus*)

The plain tiger is said to be the commonest butterfly in the world. It is found in tropical regions in South-east Asia and Africa and has recently spread to Cyprus. Its commonness may well be related to the very wide range of larval foodplants that it uses. Mostly these are in the family Asclepiadaceae, where some 25 different genera are represented. The commonly grown *Asclepias curassavica* and *A. syriaca* are among some 10 species used in that genus. Some of the foodplant records are unfortunately not precise with regard to actual species, but it does seem that even some succulent members of the family, such as *Hoya* species, can be used as well as the climbing *Tweedia caerulea*.

D. chrysippus is a rather delicate butterfly with a leisurely flight. The wing markings differ very much between the forms of this species. In Africa, for example, there are four main patterns, some being mainly orange on both fore and hind wings and others having large areas of white. These forms are mimicked by four forms of the females of *Hypolimnas missipus* and by *Acraea encedon*. The males of *D. chrysippus* can easily be distinguished from the females because they have an additional dark spot on the hind wing (a small circle when seen from underneath). The male has hair pencils which it can extrude prior to mating and these give off a pheromone. The females may select males on the basis of this pheromone, which is derived from the alkaloids taken in by the adults. The adults visit a wide range of flowers including *Lantana camara*, *Pentas lanceolata* and members of the Asteraceae (=Compositae) such as the African and French marigolds. They will, in addition, suck up the juices from fruit and are particularly fond of oranges.

Plain tigers are happy to pair and lay eggs in the tropical greenhouse. Under warm conditions, the ova hatch in four or five days. The larvae are boldly striped and have three pairs of thin fleshy appendages which they wave about when disturbed. The larval stage lasts about 14 days and the pupal stage about 11 days in a warm greenhouse. The length of the life-cycle is very much affected by temperature and this explains why there may be many generations per year in hot climates and only one in the cooler extremes of its natural range. The species is quite prolific, but in the wild a large number of the ova are taken by ants and you should guard against this in the greenhouse. An adequate food supply is probably the main concern, although they do not eat as much as *D. plexippus*.

Monarch (*Danaus plexippus*)

The monarch, or milkweed butterfly as this species is sometimes known, is generally thought of as a North American species, but it is also to be found in various places around the world as far away as South-east Asia, New Zealand and Australia. In some cases, it is present due to human activity rather than natural dispersal. Records of it in the United Kingdom may well be due to a combination of the two factors. One of its foodplants, *Asclepias curassavica*, is a common weed in tropical countries. The monarch is certainly a strong flier and is the butterfly that migrates over the longest distances. It should be noted that there are several subspecies of *D. plexippus*, not all of which migrate. The over-wintering roosts, where millions congregate in a small area, are a well-known spectacular natural phenomenon.

Pairing in this species does not appear to need the presence of the male pheromones that are essential in many danaid species. Mating flights are boistrous, and more delicate butterfly species may be knocked to the ground and even killed. Many ova are laid, normally hatching in about five days to give very hungry larvae. These grow to a large size over as little as 10 to 14 days. The pupal stage lasts about a week. It is said that if

*The monarch (*Danaus plexippus*) is a large and spectacular butterfly.*

the larvae are able to bask in the sun, the larval stage is greatly reduced in length. The larvae eat a great deal of foodplant. Mostly these are in the family Asclepiadaceae, with some 32 species in the genus *Asclepias* alone. One classical research paper records the use of cabbage (*Brassica* species) as a foodplant, but it should be noted that this was achieved by selective breeding and it is very unlikely that a stock reared on *Asclepias* species will take to cabbage.

The giant wood nymph (Idea leuconoe) *is a good butterfly for the living tropical greenhouse, but it is difficult to obtain the necessary larval foodplants.*

Striped blue crow (*Euploea mulciber*)

The striped blue crow is considered to be the most attractive of the crows, although it is only the female that is striped while the male has the best blue. It is a common species in South-east Asia, from India right through to the Philippines. The males readily extend their hair pencils from the tips of their abdomens and when present in large enough numbers are said to scent the air with the odour of their pheromones. The males will visit salty patches as well as the more usual heliotrope, stachytarpheta and composite flowers. The adults are mimicked by several unrelated species.

The larval foodplants include *Nerium oleander* (family Apocyanaceae) and *Ficus benjamina* (Moraceae) but not the species of *Asclepias* used by the *Danaus* species. They are also said to eat an unspecified species of *Aristolochia*. The pupae are very attractive, with a mirror-like gold-green surface. The exact way in which ordinary light is modified by the complex structure of the pupal case has been the subject of much study.

Common crow (*Euploea core*)

The common crow is indeed common, being found from India and China through South-east Asia to Australia and even Christmas Island. The adults are long-lived and able to recover well from accidental knocks. The flight is leisurely, but the butterflies are not particularly attractive to humans, being dull brown in colour with some white spotting. They have a fondness for withered and damaged plants that contain alkaloids, such as heliotrope and *Senecio* species, and they will visit flowers for nectar. Males often fly with the abdomen curved down and the pheromone-producing hair pencils showing at the tip of the abdomen. This species is known to migrate and also forms over-wintering roosts.

The larvae of the common crow are marked with a ring pattern and have four pairs of fleshy appendages.

The foodplants on which the larvae thrive and grow come from a wide range of families and include *Nerium oleander* (Apocyanaceae), *Asclepias curassavica* (Asclepiadaceae) and many *Ficus* species (Moraceae) such as *F. benjamina*.

Giant wood nymph (*Idea leuconoe*)

The giant wood nymph is one of the largest danaids in wingspan, but retains a papery delicacy that makes it particularly attractive. Despite its large size, it copes well in a tropical greenhouse because its flight is slow and gliding and although thin, the wings are quite tough. The bold black and white pattern is also quite distinctive. The species is widespread in South-east Asia, and several geographical races are known. The pupae require a very humid and warm atmosphere if the adults are to emerge successfully. One way to achieve this is to suspend the stick on which the pupae are attached about 15cm (6in) above a dish of warm water. The water needs to be changed from time to time and should be covered with a fine wire mesh in case the emerging butterfly should lose its footing.

The adults can live for many weeks and will visit a wide variety of flowers including heliotropes, buddleias and oleander. They also like a special feeding mixture and one formula consists of banana, natural yoghurt mixed with fruit sugar (fructose) and pure apple or orange juice.

The larval foodplants are very limited: two species of *Parsonsia* (*P. helicandra* and *P. spiralis*, family Apocyanaceae), *Cynanchum formosanum* and *Tylophora hispida* (both Asclepiadaceae). The adults can live for many weeks and you will often see them pairing, although this may depend on the presence of suitable alkaloid-containing plants, such as heliotrope. They will visit many different flowers for nectar. A single small batch of pupae will sometimes contain only one sex and, as with many other butterflies, one sex often emerges well before the other. It is generally considered that males need to be older than females for succesful mating. Unfortunately the larval foodplants are very difficult to obtain and it appears that related plants in the same genera do not stimulate egg laying, even when pairing has taken place. The different strains of *I. leuconoe* may well have distinct foodplant preferences.

HELICONIDS

Heliconids may be a family in their own right or a subfamily of the Nymphalidae. It is debatable whether or not to include the Asiatic lacewing butterflies (species of the genus *Cethosia*), but in this book we have included them with the nymphalids. The various heliconid species show a considerable range of colours and patterns. Some show an affinity with the patterning of fritillaries, while others are boldly marked with red, black, yellow and all manner of combinations of these and other colours. The common name for the heliconids is the 'longwings' due to the shape of their wings.

It is generally considered that there are about 70 different species of heliconid butterflies. Hybrid forms can occur between a few of them, but what is more remarkable is the enormous variations in patterning on the wings within some of the individual species, such as *Heliconius erato* and *H. melpomene*. All the colour forms within a species, although they are normally distinct and have probably arisen due to geographic isolation, can interbreed and produce offspring, often showing unusual pattern combinations. Not only do *H. erato* and *H. melpomene* have multiple forms which can also look almost identical on superficial examination, but these two species do not interbreed. Either these butterflies can see something we cannot or they do not use visual appearance alone when searching for a mate.

The genus *Heliconius* is said to be the most intelligent of the butterflies. As well as sight, they have a complex system of pheromones which not only covers species and mate recognition, but probably also roosting and oviposition sites. The biologist Henry Walter Bates, famed for his work on what is now called Batesian mimicry, observed

*One colour form of the postman (*Heliconius melpomene*).*

them in the Amazonian region of South America, but they do extend to Central America and three species occur in the southern United States. Many of the species are active under warm conditions even when the sun is obscured by clouds, although they can be seen at rest soaking up the sun if it is out. Many species, such as *H. erato* and *H. melpomene*, are particularly suitable for a small greenhouse and can be bred continuously all the year round.

The adults are almost all medium-sized butterflies with quite small bodies and the larvae do not, individually, consume large amounts of foodplant, although some of them, such as *Dryas julia*, can be prolific. Many of the species have an active adult life of many weeks or even months. Those that live a long time also lay their ova a few at a time over a long period, so that there are normally all stages of the life-cycle present. On the wing, the adults mostly have a relaxed, wheeling flight that helps them to avoid obstacles and they usually remain in very good condition for their age.

The passion flower family (Passifloraceae) provides the food for the larvae of heliconids. If you are breeding heliconids, you should consult a book which gives a detailed account of these plants. Not all of the species used in the wild are readily available. In some cases, you can substitute one species for another, but there are a few heliconids that are very restricted in their larval foodplants. Studies are complicated by the fact that plants can sometimes have the incorrect name on them or may be hybrids that look like one species but actually carry some of the characteristics of another. Most butterfly-plant interactions are of a biochemical nature and this is something that is often not known even by an experienced grower.

A supply of pollen is essential for the well-being of almost all heliconid species. The butterflies collect the pollen by rubbing their proboscis against the anthers. The pollen collects along the length of the proboscis and the butterflies can reach all parts of the pollen masses by uncoiling this specialized mouthpart. Experiments indicate that adults do not live very long in the absence of pollen, nor are the females very prolific. Clearly, there are nutrients in the pollen that they need, so you should make sure there are a lot of

flowers available whenever heliconids are flying. In the winter, when flowers are in short supply, it may be necessary to obtain a source of dry pollen from a suitable commercial supplier. Pollen is normally available as dry granules that require crushing in a pestle and mortar before being placed in a small dish.

Heliconids do not lay their ova just anywhere in the greenhouse. If the location of the plant, the angle of the sun at the right time of day or the condition of the plant is not correct, many species will not lay ova at all. Others may cram the ova on to a small part of just one plant that provides the right conditions. Heliconid ova are not robust and may be eaten by ants, dry up or overheat. The larvae are subject to the same problems, as well as attack by spiders. It can be difficult to remove the ova from a plant without damaging them. Female heliconids generally only lay a few ova each day, so keeping them alive for a long

The underside of the Gulf fritillary (Agraulis vanillae) *showing the bold silver patches.*

time is important. Interactions within and between species may also inhibit a female from laying ova. She may be put off by scent left by members of the same or other species of heliconid, or if she sees ova on the plant. Some species of *Passiflora* have small yellow swellings on their stipules (small outgrowths occuring at the base of the stalk of the leaf) that resemble heliconid ova and these are said to be an adaptation to deter heliconids from laying on the plants.

Heliconid larvae are spiny all over, even on the head capsule. Some people find the spines can irritate their skin, but others seem unaffected by contact with the larvae. The basic body colour is whitish in some species, but distinctly brownish or even multi-coloured in others. Although the larvae do not vary much in body size, the amount eaten by the larvae can vary. The pre-pupal stage of those larvae with whitish bodies is generally quite obvious, because they turn a pale brown colour and start to wander about. They may pupate on the foodplant, perhaps hanging from the tip of a tendril, or at some distance from the foodplant. The pupae of the more evolutionarily advanced species have various spines on them, while those considered more primitive are generally smooth. Some pupae have a few bright gold spots on them, but the general colour is brownish or mottled.

Gulf fritillary (*Agraulis vanillae*)

This species is sometimes attributed to the genus *Dione* and is often found in the wild with *Dione juno*. The common name of Gulf fritillary reflects the fact that it is found all around the Gulf of Mexico and well into South America. The adult butterfly has a number of silver patches on the underside, while small darker rings and spots occur on the brownish-orange upper surfaces. They do not collect pollen and the adults live only a short time, but fly very actively. They lack warning coloration. Among the plants used for oviposition are *Passiflora ligularis* and *P. auriculata* and even some strains of *P. foetida*, a plant that is normally avoided by heliconids. The larvae are clothed with rather short spines and have a dark, almost black colour. Large numbers can be destructive to passion flower plants.

*A silver spotted flambeau (*Dione juno*) on* Pentas lanceolata *flowers.*

Silver spotted flambeau (*Dione juno*)

This butterfly has a similar underside to *Agraulis vanillae*, with silver patches, but it has darker bands rather than spots on the upper surface. Its common name of the silver spotted flambeau links it more to *Dryas julia*, but it is certainly more like the Gulf fritillary in its habits, being short-lived and a rapid flyer. Unusually for a heliconid, the ova are laid in groups and are red, but typically will hatch within a week. The larvae feed communally and should not be separated or disturbed as they then become disorientated and may cease to feed. The larvae are light brown with short spines and a dark head. Feeding lasts for about three weeks and the pupal stage for about 10 days. The species can be very prolific and become a pest on passion fruit farms in South and Central America. Many different species of *Passiflora* are used as larval foodplants, including *P. edulis*, *P. vitifolia*, *P. alata* and *P. platyloba*.

Flambeau (*Dryas julia*)

This species is sometimes written as *Dryas iulia*, but many people find it easier to pronounce with a 'j'. It has the common name of flambeau (or flame) due to its brilliant orange colour when it has just emerged. Unlike the species of the genus *Heliconius*, *D. julia* flies rapidly in a style that has been compared to that of a dragonfly, with rapid changes of direction. Experts distinguish several different subspecies and the amount of darker banding on the wings is quite variable. The species occurs from the southern United States well into South America. The life-span of the adult is generally shorter than that of *Heliconius* species and the rich colour of the newly emerged adults does become quite dull. They visit various flowers including the greenhouse favourites, lantanas and pentas.

A search among old, brown tendrils generally reveals a single ovum of *D. julia* on each one, although the ova are sometimes laid in other obscure places. On emerging, the larvae seek mid to older leaves. Each one eats a thin strip which then hangs down, with the larva at the tip of it. In a greenhouse, this can be a very prolific species and numbers can build up rapidly to devastating proportions, eating all available leaves.

The larvae are easily recognized by their dark

One of the most distinctive heliconids, the Zebra (Heliconius charitonius).

brownish red patchy skin, with some lighter areas, and substantial spines. Almost any species of *Passiflora* may be eaten, including the common *P. caerulea*, *P. biflora*, *P. rubra*, *P. sanguinolenta*, *P. suberosa* and others. The larval stage lasts about three weeks. The pupa is of the more primitive type, without spines and a rather mottled, but variable, coloration. Emergence from the pupa can occur in 10 to 12 days in warm conditions.

Zebra (*Heliconius charitonius*)

The dramatic black coloration of the wings, with bright lemon-yellow stripes makes this one of the most easily recognized of heliconids and gives rise to its common name of zebra. This is a very common species, ranging from the southern United States, through Central to South America, and it is another prolific species if the right conditions are available. It is a classic example of a butterfly which engages in communual roosting, where large numbers congregate together in

A flambeau (Dryas julia) *with very few dark markings on the wings.*

one small area. Each hangs down from a suitable perch, such as the tip of a tendril, and there can be quite a struggle for the most favoured sites. It is thought that this is a protective mechanism for the species, with only the outliers being most vulnerable to predators. A roosting site is scent marked and may be kept for many days before it is suddenly changed for a new one, and it is better not to disturb the plants that have been chosen for roosting. The females use pheromones to attract the males. The males are generally older than the females, even to the extent that a female that is about to emerge from its pupa will be mobbed as, or even before, it emerges. Adult zebras should live for many weeks, given a supply of pollen.

Female zebras mostly lay their ova on shoot tips and these can often accumulate large numbers of ova. This is something that is not seen with most heliconid species. After they hatch, the larvae feed at first on the tips of tendrils and young leaves. Older larvae have a white body with black spines, but are distinguishable from those of *H. melpomene* by the presence of a white rather than a yellowish head capsule. Foodplants include the common *Passiflora caerulea*, *P. rubra*, *P. suberosa*, *P. bryanoides* and *P. morifolia*. The last is a strong plant with large leaves that is not eaten by many other heliconid species. The larval stage can last about three weeks and the pupae are of the 'advanced' type with spines and a characteristic pair of long 'ears' at the head end. Adults emerge from the pupae in about 12 days. There is some debate as to whether the second term of the scientific name should be *charitonius* or *charitonia*, but that need not concern us here.

Small postman *(Heliconius erato)*

This species looks like a slightly smaller version of *H. melpomene* which is how it earned its common name of the small postman. The colouring and patterns on the wings vary considerably in the many subspecies and those with a blue coloration on the upper surface, especially of the hindwings, are particularly attractive. *H. erato* can be distinguished from *H. melpomene* by the presence of four small red spots visible on the underside of the wings close to the body where *H. melpomene* has only three. Interbreeding does not occur between the two species, but does between the subspecies within a species.

The small postman's natural range is from Mexico through Panama to the Amazon basin.

The intensity of the blue coloration on the upper side of the wings of this small postman (Heliconius erato) *varies with the direction of the light.*

H. erato is not as prolific as *H. melpomene* and is generally more difficult to establish as a self-perpetuating colony. This may be because its preferred larval foodplants, such as *Passiflora biflora*, *P. rubra*, *P. sanguinolenta* and *P. coreacea* are less commonly grown. The plant called *Passiflora talamancensis* is used in the wild by *H. erato* but is rarely cultivated except by a few specialist growers of passion flowers.

Golden helicon (*Heliconius hecale*)

The golden helicon is one of the larger heliconids and there is a lot of variation in the colour and patterning of the wings. Some of these are mimicked by other species, such as *H. hecalesia* and ithomiids of the genus *Tithorea*. One form has dark brownish forewings with many lighter spots and paler brown hindwings with some darker banding. The natural range of this common species is from Peru to Mexico and it has been reported to be migratory. The ova are laid singly on leaves or tendrils. The foodplants include *P. auriculata*, *P. x belotii* (a cross between *P. alata* and *P caerulea*), *P. oerstedii*, *P. manicata*, *P. platyloba* and *P. vitifolia*. Some people find it a difficult species to establish in the greenhouse.

Postman (*Heliconius melpomene*)

This species is particularly suitable for the living tropical greenhouse, because there are many distinct and very colourful subspecies and a great variety of patterns on the wings. A frequently seen form has a predominantly black upper surface to the wings with a red band across the forewing, giving it the common name of postman, although that reference will not be readily understood except by people of a certain age and country. The flight is leisurely and under favourable conditions,

A golden helicon (Heliconius hecale) *probing a flower of* Pentas lanceolata *with its proboscis.*

and a supply of pollen, the adults should enjoy a long life.

In the wild, the species is found in many parts of Central and South America, with the individual subspecies generally restricted to just a few regions because where they mix there is no barrier to cross-pairing. Pairing takes place readily and ova, usually laid in the late afternoon, are to be found a few at a time on the young growth. They may take as little as three to five days to hatch. The larvae have a white body with black spines and a yellowish head capsule that distinguishes

A common form of the postman (Heliconius melpomene).

them from the larvae of *H. charitonius. Passiflora caerulea* is taken as a larval foodplant in the greenhouse, but several others are also eaten, such as *P. ambigua, P. x belotii, P.oerstedii, P. manicata* and others. The pupal stage lasts only about two weeks and in appearance the pupa is of the 'advanced' type with spines, but lacking the ears of *H. charitonius*. They are similar to, but a little smaller than, the pupae of *H. hecale*.

Small blue Grecian (*Heliconius sara*)
The small blue Grecian derives its name from the rich blue coloration seen on the uppersides of the wings, which are also crossed by two whitish bars on the forewings. The upperside of the hindwings may also have whitish 'piano-key' markings at its edge. The species ranges from the Amazon basin to Mexico but is only found in localities where its natural foodplant, *P. auriculata*, is growing. This is not an easy species to breed because of the requirement for a particular species of *Passiflora* for oviposition, although the larvae are said also to eat *P. biflora*. The adults use their proboscis to collect pollen loads and the females lay their ova in groups on young shoot tips.

Scarce bamboo page (*Philaethria dido*)
At first sight this does not appear to be a heliconid butterfly at all because of the bold green patterning on the upperside of the wings. The forewings are somewhat elongated, however, and the larval foodplants are all species of *Passiflora* being quoted as *P. edulis, P. vitifolia* and *P. ambigua*. Unusually, old leaves are chosen for oviposition. Although the larvae are similar to other heliconids in structure, they are quite distinctly multi-coloured. The pupae are even simpler than those of *Dryas julia* and have the appearance of bird droppings. The life-span is rather short and adults do not collect pollen on their proboscis. The adults look very similar to the nymphalid *Siproeta stelenes*, whose larvae feed on totally different plants. The flight of the scarce bamboo page is fast and they prefer to go as high as possible, making them difficult to maintain and breed in a small greenhouse, despite their very attractive appearance.

*The small blue Grecian (*Heliconius sara*) is a very attractive and distinct species of heliconid.*

*The scarce bamboo page (*Philaethria dido*) is a heliconid with unusual coloration.*

ITHOMIIDS

This family, or as some prefer, subfamily within the Nymphalidae, contains butterflies found in tropical regions of Central and South America. Some experts include the genus *Tellervo* with the ithomiids, but this comes from the Old World and for various reasons can be considered quite

The glasswing (Greta oto) *pairs easily under the right conditions.*

commonly called glasswings. In all species, the abdomen is very thin and only two pairs of legs are used for walking.

In all species, the males have distinct, hair-like scales on the front margins of the hindwings. These can be erected and give off a pheromone which is probably derived from substances taken in by the adults from poisonous plants, such as the heliotrope. The pheromones of different species may be the same and the males of many species may collect together in large groups called leks. It is thought that the pheromones attract females, and perhaps even other males, to the lek. Most ithomiids are forest species and fly in quite dull light. It is generally assumed that the ithomiids are quite closely related to the danaids, and certainly they have some features in common between them.

Most of the larval foodplants are in the potato family (Solanaceae) with a few from the oleander family (Apocyanaceae). The larval foodplants of quite a few species are not known or have not been fully identified beyond the genus level. Although these two families contain many poisonous plants, it is thought that the adults obtain their protection more from the plants that they visit, such as species of *Heliotropium*, *Myosotis* (both Boraginaceae), *Senecio* and *Eupatorium* (both Asteraceae=Compositae). This is also the source of the precursors for the male pheromones and these may be essential for mating. If these plants are not growing in the greenhouse, bunches with roots should be hung up. It does not matter that they are not growing or are drying up, but they do need to be sprayed with water occasionally.

distinct. The taxonomy and identification of the ithomiids are complex matters. There are probably about 45 distinct genera and around 300 different species, but the situation is complicated by the fact that there are a great number of species which mimic one another. The markings on the wings match one another so closely that to tell between them you have to study details such as the venation of the hindwings. They are mostly small, delicate-looking butterflies with wingspans in the region of 2.5–11cm (1–4 1/2in). The patterns range from amber backgrounds, through tiger-striped and blotched, to species with predominantly transparent wings, these last being

Glasswing (*Greta oto*)

This is a typical glasswing ithomiid and generally the species most readily available for breeding. It is quite widely distributed in Central America from Mexico to Panama and on some of the islands. Despite its small size and apparent fragility, it can fly long distances and is considered to be a genuine migratory species. Generally, however, they are to be seen making short flights between one plant and another, pausing to probe the surface with their proboscis, or at flowers and ripe fruit. They are a good species for a tropical greenhouse and it is quite easy to establish a breeding population. Many species of the genus *Cestrum* (Solanaceae), such as *C. nocturnum*, *C. parqui* and *C.* 'Newellii' are larval foodplants, but there is a definite preference for those which do not have very hairy leaves.

As would be expected from a butterfly that has a small abdomen and lives a long time, the ova are laid over a long period of time, mostly only one or two per leaf, if sufficient leaves are available. The ova are round and whitish and the newly hatched larvae eat small holes out of the centre of the leaves. Older larvae are basically pale green with some whitish and yellowish striping along the body, which is not hairy or spiny. Ova and larvae are very vulnerable to ant predation. The pupa is an amazing shape, much shortened and compressed. The colouring bears a resemblance to that of danaids and is usually described as chrome coloured, although it has also been described as iridescent green. They are quite loosely attached to the underside of leaves and sometimes fall off. Unlike most butterflies, the adults seem to be able successfully to extract themselves from such unattached pupae and expand their wings normally.

Morphos

Undoubtedly the most dramatic of the South American butterflies, the morphos are noted for their large size and the brilliant blue coloration of the upperside of the wings. Not all species, nor even the females of some species where the male is iridescent, have this bright blue coloration. Neither are all the species large; wingspans range from 7 to 25cm (3 to 10in). The undersides are generally a dull brown, with complex patterning and eyespots. The blue and other bright colours on the wings are due to refraction of light rather than actual blue pigments. These colours may serve to attract mates, and the sudden change from brown to bright blue may also deter some predators. As is the situation with so many butterflies, there is considerable disagreement between experts on the number of species that exist; there may be anything between 40 and 80. Some put only the genus *Morpho* in the family, but others also add *Antirrhea* and *Caerois*, while another contingent consider morphos to be a subfamily in the Nymphalidae.

The adults do not visit flowers, but feed instead on rotting fruit and fungi. Males often feed in small groups and may even roost together, but at other times they will be solitary in habit. The larval foodplants of the genus *Morpho* are mostly in the families Fabaceae (=Leguminosae) and Mimosaceae. The ova are unusual in being hemispherical and in some species are laid singly while in others small batches are more frequent. The larvae are very hairy, often quite brightly coloured and have two, generally short, tails to the last segment. The larvae can emit a strong

Morpho butterflies normally perch with closed wings. The blue coloration only shows in flight.

odour when provoked and it has been shown that some species also possess a gland on their back which exudes a drop of liquid just after moulting. This is taken on to the hairs on the head capsule and then spread all over the body. The pupae of the genus *Morpho* are roughly ovoid and lack any prominent ornamentation. Although many of the larval foodplants are poisonous there is doubt as to whether or not the adults are distasteful to any significant extent.

Common morpho (*Morpho peleides*)

This species is the one most often available for breeding and it prefers to fly fairly near the ground. Many other species are essentially canopy dwellers and require a very large greenhouse. *M. peleides* is of medium size, with a wingspan of 13–16cm (5–6in). The amount of blue on the wings varies a great deal and several subspecies are described, some with very little blue at all. The males and females have quite different habits. The males are active in the morning, while the females are out only around midday. There are extrudable hairs on the male abdomen, near the claspers, which are said to give off a vanilla-like scent. The undersides of the wings are a dull brown with various markings and eyespots.

The ova are laid on a wide range of plants, such as species of *Mucuna*, *Dalbergia* and *Pterocarpus* and there some additional ones that the larvae will eat, such are *Arachis hypogaea* (the peanut). The ova are greenish white, with a touch of red on the 'lid'. The larvae are hairy and generally yellow at first and red later, developing more complex patterning with more brownish tinges. The pupae are greenish, usually with a few bright shiny spots. There is no diapause. The adults, if fed with plenty of rotting fruit and sugar water, can live for a long time.

NYMPHALIDS

The nymphalids are one of the largest groups of butterflies with several thousand species. Species that resemble one another are generally grouped together and have common names such as fritillaries, admirals and emperors. Representatives of the nymphalids can be found in all parts of the globe, but many of the genera are restricted to tropical regions. The range of wing shape and patterning is enormous, some being cryptically coloured while others have brilliant markings. Many species are only active in bright light, when they may have a strong, rapid flight, and for this reason require quite a large flight area. Some of the most familiar European temperate zone butterflies are actually nymphalids which migrate from warmer climates during the summer months.

Malay lacewing (*Cethosia hypsea*)

The Malay lacewing derives its common name both from its country of origin and the delicate patterning on the underside of the wings. This pattern varies from one species of *Cethosia* to another. Most of the upperside of the hindwing and part of the forewing are a bright orange in the males and a slightly yellower shade in the females, with a broad

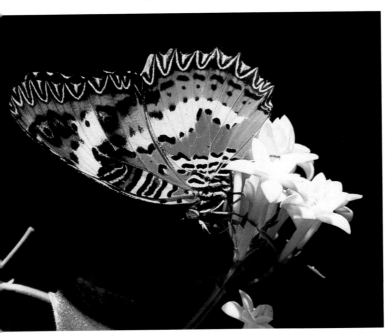

The complex markings of the underside of the wings of Cethosia hypsea, *here on bouvardia flowers, give rise to its common name of lacewing.*

edge of brown and some whitish markings. Related species range from India and throughout South-east Asia.

The lacewings are sometimes grouped with the heliconids and their larvae do feed on members of the Passifloraceae. The ova are laid in small batches on tendrils or around young shoots and the young larvae feed together. With their bright red colouring and whitish saddle mark they are very obvious, but should not be disturbed nor separated. There is some doubt as to the preferred foodplant for this species, possibly because of different strains. Ova have been laid on *Passiflora caerulea*, and *Adenia* species are also quoted as larval foodplants. The pupa is quite angular and attached by the tail.

*A male great eggfly (*Hypolimnas bolina*).*

Great eggfly (*Hypolimnas bolina*)

The great eggfly has many different colour forms, particularly in the females, and many subspecies have been named. It has a wide distribution in South-east Asia, from India through to Papua New Guinea and Australia. The common name is probably derived from the fact that the females lay batches of ova on a wide range of plants, particularly members of the Acanthaceae and Urticaceae families. They will lay on the common stinging nettle, *Urtica dioica*, but this is likely only to be a weed in the tropical greenhouse. The sweet potato (*Ipomoea batatus*) and the common large bindweed (*Calystegia sepium*), both members of the family Convolvulaceae, and *Sida rhombifolia* (Malvaceae) are also frequently named foodplants, making this a truly polyphagous species. The male generally has one large bluish spot on the upperside of each wing and white patches. Some females may be almost black and probable mimics of *Euploea* species, and others resemble *Danaus chrysippus*. Both are unpalatable danaids, so looking like them presumably gives the female eggflies some protection.

H. bolina is a strong flier, and known to be migratory on occasion. Although the males tend

*One form of the female great eggfly (*Hypolimnas bolina*).*

to chase away other males during daylight hours, they may still roost together at night. It is likely that the spots on the wings of the males help them to recognize other males rather than attract females. The adults will visit flowers, but are also attracted to fermenting fruit. When temperatures are low they will not move and can only be stimulated into activity by raising the temperature.

Gaudy commadore (*Junonia (=Precis) octavia*)

The gaudy commadore is an African member of a genus whose species occur from America to Australia and as a group are called 'pansies'. Although the males and females of *J. octavia* are almost identical in appearance, there are two distinct colour forms which occur at different times of the year. This is known as polyphenism, in contrast to polymorphism where different colour forms occur at the same time. Although the shape of the two forms is similar, the colour is so different that they were at first thought to be two different species. This difference is now known to be due to temperature and there is a reddish wet-season form and a blue dry-season form. You might think that the heat of the dry season was responsible for the blue colour of the adults, but it is actually the temperature at which the larvae develop that controls the colour. Larvae reared at around 30°C (86°F) produce red adults while those reared at around 16°C (60°F) become blue adults.

The mated females readily lay ova on the well-known variegated forms of coleus and also on *Plectranthus* species (both Lamiaceae). The larvae are patterned with dark markings and are very spiny. They consume a considerable amount of

*A gaudy commadore (*Junonia octavia)*, reared at high temperatures, on a lantana plant.*

foodplant and many large plants are required. Great care should be taken if these have been bought from an external supplier, because they are likely to have been sprayed with insecticide. The larvae are also said to show different forms, but only one is likely to occur at a time. The species is continuously brooded and there is no diapause.

Small leopard (*Phalanta phalanta*)

The small leopard occurs from Africa through India and South-east Asia to Australia. Both sexes are orange-brown with thin dark lines along the wing margins and a scattering of small dark spots. The adults are very active and the wings are constantly in motion, even when the butterfly has perched. They visit flowers, but are also attracted to mud patches. They lay their ova on a wide range of plants, including willows (*Salix* species), *Populus alba* and many tropical plants that are rarely available in temperate regions, such as *Flacourtia indica* and *Trimeria grandifolia* (both Flacourtiacae). Under warm greenhouse conditions, the larvae develop very quickly and a considerable quantity of foodplant is needed to satisfy them. You should, of course, exercise great care when bringing in any additional foodplant from outside the greenhouse, because plant pests can easily be introduced on plants that have not been 'quarantined' correctly.

PAPILIONIDS

Although the family Papilionidae is probably one of the most studied of all butterfly groups, there is still much doubt as to how many species there are, with estimates varying from around 575 to 700. Even in this family our knowledge is far from complete. The adults are mostly vigorous butterflies with a strong flight, often hovering when they are feeding at flowers.

Although the common name of these butterflies is swallowtails, not all of the species have the characteristic tails, and in some cases males and females of the same species differ in this respect. Some of the species are too large to fly well in a small flight area and many require more larval foodplant to support a colony than can be grown in a small greenhouse. They often

*The small leopard (*Phalanta phalanta*) is a modest-sized but active butterfly.*

need direct sunlight for active flight and feeding, and there may not be much activity on dull days. This can be important, because the life-span of the adults is not usually more than a couple of weeks.

The majority of the swallowtail species belong to the subfamily Papilioninae and most live in the tropics. The remaining three subfamilies are not discussed further here, because the largest, Parnassiinae, with some 50 species, are all non-tropical and of the other two, one is entirely fossil and the other has a single living species that is not usually available for breeding. The largest swallowtails are the birdwings, all protected and many endangered, although some can be relatively easily bred, provided sufficient space and foodplants are available. None would be suitable for a small domestic greenhouse. Among the smallest swallowtails are *Lamproptera* species, with a wingspan of about 50mm (2in). The remainder are medium to large butterflies of striking appearance. It may seem strange to those

of us in temperate climates to learn that some swallowtails are considered to be pests. This is because their larvae feed on the leaves of the commercially important species of the genus *Citrus*, although they may also eat other cultivated members of the Rutaceae family. There are, of course, many members of the Rutaceae that are not grown as crops and so these provide alternative natural larval foodplants for many swallowtails. A second major group of swallowtail species has larvae that feed on leaves of the pipevines, which are poisonous plants in the family Aristolochiaceae.

Papilionid females tend to lay their ova quite soon after pairing, due no doubt to their relatively short active life. During this time, they need plenty of flowers for nectar, as well as good lighting conditions. The citrus-feeding swallowtails usually choose young leaves for oviposition and the ova may be quite crowded if there are not many suitable leaves. If suitable sites are available, the ova are spread widely over many different plants. Many of the pipevine-feeding species lay their ova on older leaves or even alongside the foodplants rather than on it. The ova are normally rounded and if they are not stuck down too firmly they can be removed, if necessary, from all but the softest leaves. Hatching can take place in as little as a few days for some species, but a week or more for others.

Larval development, however, is not always synchronized within one batch of ova and pupae may form over a long period. This means that where there is no diapause period, some adults may have emerged before other larvae have completed their development. This may occur especially when using alternative foodplants rather than the best one for the particular butterfly species. Some larvae, particularly those of the pipevine-feeding species, develop fleshy outgrowths from the body. Larvae with white saddle markings are considered to indicate that a species is more primitive, in an evolutionary sense. In many species there are structures called osmetaria that can be extruded from the larval body when it is approached. These give off a strong odour that is said to be a deterrent, but

A tailed jay *(*Graphium agamemnon*) with wings open.*

many larvae depend more upon a resemblance to bird droppings to avoid predation. Where alternative larval foodplants are given in books, it should be remembered that this does not mean that the larvae will change at any time from one plant species to another. You may also find that the vitality of the stock decreases after a few generations bred on alternative foodplants, such as *Choisya ternata*, while those reared on *Citrus* species do not have this problem. The larvae of pipevine swallowtails can be very destructive to foodplants, because they often eat through the stems, causing whole shoots to wilt and die. Thus they deprive other larvae and themselves of food.

When pre-pupal larvae have selected a spot for pupation, they spin a silk pad at the site near to each side of the body and make a girdle of silken threads around themselves, as well as the normal pad at the tail end. The girdle can sink into the pupal case while it is still soft and become firmly fixed there. If a larva chooses an unsuitable position, you should cut off these attachments close to the pad before you make any attempt to remove a pupa. If a removed pupa is stuck to an emergence stick in the normal manner by the tail end alone, emergence will be quite satisfactory. Just a few of the swallowtail species that are sometimes available for breeding are briefly discussed below, but they represent a reasonable range of types.

Pipevine swallowtail (*Atrophaneura polyeuctes*)
Although the scientific name is difficult to pronounce, this is an attractive member of the group known as 'black swallowtails' because of the predominant colour of the wings, although

there are bright red and white patches and sometimes clearer patches on the wings of many species. *A. polyeuctes* occurs naturally in South-east Asia and is a typical pipevine swallowtail with larvae that feed on species of *Aristolochia*. The flight is typically strong and pairing generally presents no problems. The pair fly while still joined, one carrying the other. The females lay their ova near the foodplant or on old stems, rather than on the leaves. Various *Aristolochia* species can be used as larval foodplants, including some of the smaller-leaved ones that may, or may not, have the flowers that give off a smell that is objectionable to humans.

The larval stage is typical for the pipevine swallowtails, with a dark reddish-brown colour and fleshy spines all over the body. The species is not generally very prolific and a small colony can be kept going without the need for too much foodplant, there being no diapause period. The pupae, like those of many pipevine swallowtails, are dark brown and have numerous stubby projections on them.

Tailed jay (*Graphium agamemnon*)

The first thing that you notice with this butterfly is the green on the upper surface of the wings, but this is actually a pattern of spots on a much darker background. The underside is completely different and blends into a leafy background so well that the butterfly is difficult to see when under a leaf with closed wings. There are distinct tails to the wings, which overall are shaped like a traditional-style kite, making this species a typical member of the 'kite' group of swallowtails. Unfortunately the wings of the tailed jay are quite fragile and the tips can soon become ragged. Although the natural foodplants for the larvae are mainly plants such as *Annona squamosa* and other members of the custard apple family (Annonaceae), they will also eat the leaves of some members of the magnolia family (Magnoliaceae) such as *M. stellata*, *M. x soulangiana*, *M. grandiflora* and in the wild *Michelia champaca*.

The ova hatch in about a week. The larvae are bright green in their later stages, although when young they have a rather bulbous brown front end. The larval stage takes about 30 days and the pupae are relatively large, smooth and pale green, with a spike at the head region. The pupal stage lasts about 24 days under warm conditions.

Green dragontail (*Lamproptera meges*)

The green dragontail is one of the smaller swallowtails, but it has the longest tails. It occurs widely in South-east Asia from India and China to Malaysia and elsewhere. Although a jungle species, green dragontails are found near water and their very rapid, darting flight resembles that of dragonflies. They like damp mud and will settle on it, but when visiting flowers they prefer to hover rather than settle. They fly in bright light and tend to go to the lightest parts of the greenhouse. The larval foodplant of a closely related species is *Illigera cordata* (Hernandaceae), but it has been suggested that *L. meges* might lay ova on members of the Rutaceae, such as rue.

*The green dragontail (*Lamproptera meges*) is unusual, but clearly a swallowtail butterfly.*

A butterfly that buzzes as it flies is so unusual that this species, which is only rarely available, would repay greater studies on possible alternative foodplants, although such research is not recommended for the beginner.

Mocker (*Papilio (=Princeps) dardanus*)

This papilionid from South Africa is both large and noteworthy for the fact that there are several different colour forms of the female and a single common one of the male. The male can, in any case, be easily distinguished from the female because it has tails to the hindwings which are absent in the female. Not only the wing patterns, but also the habits of the two sexes differ, the females being much more inclined to seek cover while the males are out actively flying. There are differences in the markings of wet and dry season forms. Mocker is an appropriate common name, because the female forms are classic examples of Batesian mimicry, resembling as they do various different species of distasteful danaid butterflies. In its native habitat, the larval foodplants are plants from the Rutaceae that are not common in cultivation, such as *Teclea natalensis*, *Vepris* species and *Clausena anisata* as well as cultivated

A *very pale colour form of a male mocker (*Papilio dardanus*) feeding at* Euphorbia milii *flowers.*

Citrus species. *Choisya* may be taken in the greenhouse, but citrus is preferred.

Young mocker larvae have white projections at each end of the body and are predominantly brown with white markings. The pupae are bright green with a yellow stripe along the side and sharply pointed ends. Although the species has no diapause, it can be a difficult one to breed, especially over the winter in temperate regions.

Common mormon (*Papilio polytes*)

This is one of the easiest swallowtails to breed. It is another of the black group, although there is a substantial band of white spots on the upper side of the wings of the male. The female has several different patterns, although all can interbreed with the single type of male. One form has a considerable amount of red as well as white markings on the wings and is said to mimic a common species of pipevine swallowtail, although it lacks the red body colour of its distasteful relative. Pairing takes place readily and the ova are laid on *Citrus* species, often in large numbers. The ova hatch in as little as four days. The larvae will also eat other members of the Rutaceae, such as species of *Murraya*, *Ruta*, *Skimmia* and *Choisya* and some people have recorded larvae feeding on African marigolds (*Tagetes* species in the Asteraceae). Although a few generations may be raised successfully on these alternative foodplants, it does not seem that the species can be maintained indefinitely on such plants. The larvae are not often seen moving unless disturbed and lie around on the upper surface of leaves, presumably relying on their resemblance in the earlier stages to bird droppings. Later, they become bright green and are more likely to be found along the stems. Although the length of time they spend as larvae can be quite variable, about four weeks is common. They seem to like a light position, but can desiccate if left in the sun and under too dry conditions. Because *Citrus* species tend to regenerate leaves rather slowly and because the common mormon is very prolific, problems can arise. The pupae are green or brownish, and this stage lasts about two weeks. There is no diapause.

A Chinese yellow swallowtail *(Papilio xuthus).*

Chinese yellow swallowtail (*Papilio xuthus*)

This yellow and black species has a superficial resemblance to the familiar swallowtails of similar colour that occur in temperate regions, but it comes from South-east Asia and Japan and is probably a recent immigrant to Hawaii. The pupae show a distinct winter diapause but, after a reasonable period of cool conditions, can be stimulated by warmth to complete their development earlier in the year. Without the cool rest period, the emergence of the adults will be very erratic. This can tie in well with their liking for laying ova on the young leaves of *Poncirus trifoliata*, a deciduous member of the Rutaceae. *Citrus* species are a main foodplant for the larvae in Hawaii, but other members of the Rutaceae are used in Japan. The existence of the diapause means that this is a good species for those who cannot maintain high temperatures all through the winter period.

Common parides (*Parides iphidamus*)

This South American butterfly is just one species from a genus in which the females of all the species are very similar and difficult to tell apart, while the males generally differ from one another. In *P. iphidamus*, the predominant colour of the adult is black with a broad red band on the hindwing. On the upperside of the forewing there is a large white patch in the female and a much smaller one on the male. The male has an androconial fold along the edge of the hindwing that has special white woolly scales in it. These appear to be transferred to the antennae of the

female during courtship. After mating the females are usually found to have a mating plug attached to the genital pore which prevents further mating until it has disintegrated. The males and females have different habits: the males stay in the open all the time while the females seek out suitable plants on which to lay their ova. They visit flowers, especially red ones, including *Impatiens walleriana* (=*sultani*) (Balsaminaceae),

A female common mormon (Papilio polytes) *feeding at flowers of* Stachytarpheta mutabilis.

A male common parides (Parides iphidamus*).*

a species which does not usually attract many butterflies. The larval foodplants are various species of *Aristolochia*, such as *A. triangularis* and *A. trilobata* and the larvae appear to be able to switch from one species to another quite easily. The ova are laid singly on the leaves and are a dull, brownish colour. The larvae are a dark, blackish colour with a small whitish saddle and many soft fleshy tubercles. The adults are quite long-lived and the species is continuously brooded.

PIERIDS

The family Pieridae contains well over 1,000, possibly almost 2,000, species, many of them common butterflies, and they are found in all regions of the world. Among the common group names are the whites, yellows, sulphurs, orange tips and jezebels, which gives some indication of their respective visual appearances and, to some extent, the way that the family is subdivided into three or four subfamilies. Most species belong to the subfamily Pierinae, with larvae feeding mainly on species within the plant families Brassicaceae (=Cruciferae), Capparidaceae and Loranthaceae. The other pierids feed mostly on plants in the Fabaceae, Caesalpinaceae and Mimosaceae families. The ova are generally cylindrical with ridges both along and across the surface and narrowed at the tip. They are usually laid singly but a few species lay them in groups. The larvae have short hairs and the pupae are attached to

their supports both by the tail end and by a silken girdle around the middle. A few species are pests of crops and some are genuine migrants over quite long distances. Most are small- to medium-sized adults, but a few reach 11cm (4in) in wingspan. In many tropical species, the pupal stage only lasts a few days and they are rarely available for breeding because of this.

Great orange tip (*Hebomoia glaucippe*)

The great orange tip is exactly as its name implies: large, with orange tips to the whitish wings in both sexes. The undersides are brownish and the orange tips do not show when the butterfly is at rest with its wings closed. The males often congregate at mud patches where they probably obtain salts to be passed on to the females during mating. The species is widely distributed in South-east Asia from India, through Thailand, Malaysia and elsewhere. The flowers they visit, especially the females, include *Lantana camara*. Ova are laid on members of the Capparidaceae and include *Cleome spinosa*, *Capparis moonii* and *Crataeva religiosa*. The larvae are remarkable for their threat display when disturbed. At rest they are inconspicuous, being green with a yellowish strip at the side. When disturbed, they expand the front two segments of the body, revealing two dark simulated eye-spots. This makes the larvae look like a snake's head. The pupa is pale green and not at all obvious against a leafy background.

SATYRIDS

There are between 1,500 and 3,000 species in this family (or subfamily of the Nymphalidae) and they occur in all regions of the world. Although the family is known by the common name of 'browns', this does not give a true indication of the range of patterns and colours that are shown. Eye-spots are found on the wings of many of the species while others are mimics of unrelated butterflies. In wingspan, the species range from around 2.5 to 13cm (1 to 5in). Many of the tropical species have brilliant appearances and exhibit a wide range of wing shapes. The ova are usually spherical with fine ribs, and the majority of larvae feed on members of the grass family

*A great orange tip (*Hebomoia glaucippe*) on a plant of* Cleome spinosa.

Poaceae (=Graminae). The larvae are generally greenish or brownish in colour, sometimes with stripes along the body, which is smooth. A typical larva has a bifid 'tail' and a pair of 'horns' on the head. The pupae are usually rounded and rather short and may be either attached by the tail end or lying loose at the base of plants or under stones.

Common palmfly (*Elymnias hypermnestra*)
Although predominantly brownish in colour, the common palmfly has many distinct forms in South-east Asia and many of these mimic species of danaid. In some subspecies, the males and females look the same, but in others they are quite distinct, a situation also found in other members of the genus. The habits of the subspecies may also differ, with some liking the shade and others the sun. In smaller greenhouses, palms such as *Howeia* (=*Kentia*) *forsteriana* are suitable larval foodplants, but the palm usually named for this species is coconut (*Cocos nucifera*). The date palm

(*Phoenix dactylifera*) and other palms may be equally suitable. The larvae are typical for satyrids, being greenish and with a forked tail. The species is continuously brooded and passes through the life-cycle quickly, but, because the adults are rather small, the larvae do not consume excessive quantities of foodplant.

Elymnias hypermnestra, *the common palmfly.*

12 Starting a butterfly colony

There are many things to be considered when obtaining livestock to start up a breeding colony of tropical butterflies. Obviously you must have the necessary foodplants available and the appropriate facilities. Foodplants generally need at least six months, or more, to become established, and you cannot dash out and buy them ready for immediate use. The same principle generally applies to the butterfly livestock. This is likely to be seasonally available and the supply of many species is often very erratic. In most cases, you will have to purchase your livestock, but some breeders will be happy to exchange livestock, once you have something to exchange.

The starting stage

It is possible to start a breeding colony from any of the four stages of the life-cycle, but each has its own characteristics. Ova are concentrated units of the genetic potential of a species and take up little room. When first laid they are fragile and easily damaged, but after a day or so the shell toughens up. Only a few, such as those of *Caligo* species and some papilionids, can be easily removed from the material they have been laid on. Most are so firmly attached that they can be damaged if you try to remove them. Leaves and especially small pieces of leaves soon wilt, shrivel and dry up, or go brown and start to go mouldy. The ova of tropical butterflies are not normally resting stages and the larvae inside develop to maturity in anything between 5 and 20 days, depending on species and conditions. For these reasons, ova are usually only available from a few breeders who are able to deal with such delicate material. Ova require careful packing, and protection from excessively low or high temperatures during

This Heliconius cydno *will hybridize with the postman* (Heliconius melpomene) *and breeders will usually only keep one or the other of these two species.*

transport. Nobody expects all the ova to hatch successfully and they are generally available in batches of 12 or 15.

The larvae are even more delicate than ova and even greater care is needed when transporting them. Their foodplant must be kept fresh and provision made for some gaseous exchange. In the dark, leaves give off quite a lot of carbon dioxide, which added to that from the larvae, may reach quite high concentrations and actually be more harmful than a shortage of oxygen. Availability and other problems connected with them are similar to those with ova. Larvae usually come in batches of 10 or 12.

Livestock is usually supplied as pupae. Once they have hardened for a day or two, they can be removed from their silk pads; take care to cut any silken girdle first. Tropical butterflies stay as pupae for between 5 and about 20 days, depending on temperature and species, for those that are continuously brooded. During this time, very complex changes take place inside the pupal case. Some breeders slow the developmental processes by keeping the pupae cool, but the problem with this is that the optimum conditions for this are largely unknown. It seems certain that different stages of metamorphosis are affected by temperature in different ways. Prolonged storage at too low a temperature may lead to emergence difficulties, an obviously weak imago that fails to expand its wings properly, or one that does not feed. Cold conditions during transport may cause similar problems. Some species that can be considered 'tropical' do have a diapause while in the pupal stage. This is probably induced by the daylength or conditions during larval development and such pupae may need to be stored at a temperature lower than that needed for emergence. If this is not done the adults may emerge at very erratic intervals, if at all.

Adult butterflies are occasionally available from breeders, usually for personal collection. Obviously they are very delicate and great care is needed when transporting them. They are quiescent when placed in the dark and this conserves their energy and reduces the danger of damage to the wings. Incidentally, most butterflies

The chequered or lime swallowtail (Papilio demoleus) is one of the citrus-feeding swallowtails that is frequently available and easy to breed.

are able to fly quite well with some damage to the tips and margins of their wings; it does not adversely affect their lifespan or reproductive capability in the greenhouse. After live butterflies have been transported, it is essential to ensure that they take in some liquid to replace any that has been lost. They should, of course, have been allowed to feed before their journey.

Sources

There are basically two sources for livestock. They can come from butterfly breeding farms in tropical regions, which may, or may not, be in the natural environment of the species. These have often been set up with the dual aim of conserving local butterfly populations and providing a source of income for local people as an alternative to projects that result in habitat destruction. Transport costs and the cost of currency conversion means that this source of livestock is not generally realistic for the beginner, because large and regular orders are required. In most countries, there are a few specialist importers of livestock who supply some of the large butterfly houses and they will have small quantities of livestock available for the beginner. The preferred way of obtaining livestock is from locally bred stock, which will already have been acclimatized to the conditions that can be created in your area. The way to get in touch with breeders is to join a local society or group which has existing breeders in it and has a frequently updated 'wants and exchanges' list.

Cost

People often ask how much livestock costs? There is no simple answer to this question. It can be nothing, but it should be reasonable. If the living tropical greenhouse was properly costed as a business, it would make the cost of livestock well beyond the purchasing power of ordinary people. Nobody makes money out of breeding tropical butterflies in a temperate climate. It is a labour of love for which the rewards are personal rather than financial.

The 'market' price that you have to pay to start a colony is partly set by the amount charged for imported pupae from special butterfly farms that exist in certain tropical countries as part of their overall conservation strategies. The prices of stock bred locally in temperate climates in the type of greenhouse described in this book will fluctuate according to availability and demand, but will never reflect the full cost of producing them. Some breeders only have stock available during the warmer months, and at the start of a 'season' livestock will be more expensive than at the end. A batch of ova or young larvae will cost

about the same, but older larvae and pupae will cost more and be priced individually or as a small batch. Suppliers have no control over the livestock once you have received it and some will only consider refunds if notified within 24 hours of receipt, while others will replace or refund readily once they know you and are satisfied that you have the skill and knowledge to look after the livestock intelligently. Some require payment before dispatch, but others are happy for payment on receipt. This is best from the purchaser's point of view, because livestock ordered from a list may not be available for many weeks and sometimes not at all in a particular season. Suppliers do like to receive payment promptly and regrettably there are several who have been forced to stop supplying because customers have not paid.

Transporting livestock

If livestock is not obtained by hand-to-hand exchange, it must be transported in a suitable container. This needs to be insulated to protect the livestock inside from excessively low or high temperatures. The preferred container is one made of expanded polystyrene, with walls at least 1cm (1/2in) thick. It should be strong enough to withstand any damage caused during transport and liberal use of parcel tape will help to prevent it breaking should it suffer a blow or be crushed.

For pupae, the box is usually filled with clean cotton wool layers between which the pupae are snugly held so that they will not be shaken about.

Many butterfly species, like this Heliconius atthis, *are not generally available because their life-cycle requirements are still being investigated.*

In some cases, individual pupae may even be wrapped up in small pieces of tissue paper, especially if they are to travel long distances. If only a few pupae are being sent, a smaller plastic box can be used as the container for the pupae in their cotton wool. This inner box must be securely taped in place to prevent it moving. During hot, dry weather it is a good idea to dampen the wool with clean water to protect delicate pupae.

Larvae can also be placed in an inner plastic box, along with enough foodplant for the journey. The internal top and bottom of the box should be lined with slightly dampened tissue paper. If this inner box does not have preformed air channels, then small holes should be pierced through the lid to allow gaseous exchange between the inner box and the larger interior of the polystyrene outer box. A maximum transport time of 24 hours should be considered as the norm for larvae.

Some suppliers use cardboard boxes for the transport of pupae, again packed in cotton wool, and these are strong and generally satisfactory. No supplier can control what happens to a package once it enters the transport system and labels on a package cannot be read once it is in a bag with other items.

Species like Parthenos sylvia, *the clipper, are readily available from South-east Asia, but their foodplants are not currently available for the greenhouse breeder in temperate climates.*

In some cases, packages may be subject to quite low or high temperatures during transport. Ova are sometimes transported in a capped tube of unbreakable plastic inside a padded envelope. Thin or brittle plastic containers are very likely to get broken, even in a padded envelope.

Courier and postal services differ from country to country in terms of cost, transport times and reliability. Likewise, regulations relating to what can be transported, what containers are permitted and what labelling may be required also differ.

Legislation

There are many laws relating to butterflies. Some of these are international, such as the CITES lists, and others differ from one country to another. What may be permitted in one country may be against the law in another. There are basically three types of legislation. One concerns what can be legally in a person's possession in a particular country. A second concerns what may be legally exported from a country and this may be different from the species involved in the first type. Thirdly, there are restrictions on what can be brought into a country, because of fears that a species might become a pest. It is beyond the scope of this book to consider the complexities of such legislation, the manner in which permits can be obtained and the actual species listed in such legislation. The species described in this book are, at the time of writing, allowed species in the UK, although it is against the law to release any of them into the wild. Any reputable local breeder would, of course, only supply permitted livestock.

Epilogue

*Help us to take tropical butterflies like this zebra (*Heliconius charitonius*) into the future.*

Creating a living tropical greenhouse is no different from any other art or craft. It requires the right equipment, the right knowledge and the right creative potential skills to put theory into practice. As any true craftsperson will tell you, it also takes dedication, enthusiasm and time to create something of value. For those who have read our book and have been inspired to start their own living tropical greenhouse we offer one further word of advice: you will need patience. You will not be able to create overnight what is truly a complex micro-environment and it is, indeed, a project that can never be said to be completed. Some readers may wish to stop after establishing the plants and thereby extend our knowledge of that aspect of the living tropical greenhouse. That would not be a failure, but a valuable creation in its own right. There are many avenues of pleasure and discovery to be explored just with the plants alone.

Many tropical plants belong to the category known as 'unorthodox'. This means that their seeds cannot, at the present time, be stored in the special desiccated and low-temperature conditions of those great plant genetic resources called 'seed banks', such as the one run by the UK's Royal Botanic Gardens, Kew and designated as the Millennium Seed Bank (at Wakehurst Place, West Sussex, England). It may be that the alternative approach of a user's living store could be an effective and low-cost *ex situ* conservation solution for some tropical plants. Many of these are threatened by habitat destruction and potential climatic change, but are not of any currently known commercial significance. Some of these plants would undoubtedly be of interest to those with a living tropical greenhouse as foodplants for butterfly larvae. In this book, we have tried to enlighten the reader as to just how many different species there are in some families of plants, but have only mentioned specifically a few plants that are the minimum for a living tropical greenhouse and which are mostly easily cultivated and commercially available.

We do, however, feel that there is even more to be gained by taking the second step along the path that leads to a managed ecosystem, albeit a very limited one. We suggest that the beginner starts with only one species of butterfly and nothing could be better than the postman (*Heliconius melpomene*). After a year of progress with that species, you will be free to follow any one of a myriad of pathways. If the plants are your main interest, there are many wonderful botanic gardens for the detailed study of living plants and innumerable gardens, both public and private, full of living plants. There are large and small companies and businesses devoted to growing and looking after plants, and uncountable millions of people with an interest in gardening. There is nothing comparable for insects, even for the butterflies that we humans appear to hold so dear. There are repositories of knowledge in the world's great museums and in academic establishments, many large- and small-scale conservation schemes, plus masses of legislation, together with some excellent scientific work being carried out in many places throughout the world. Unfortunately, none of this can reverse the progress of the enormous

forest fires that are currently destroying unbelievably huge areas in the tropics, the detrimental influence of climatic change due, perhaps, to global warming, or the increasing effect of human influences in land clearance, urbanization and warfare. Creating living tropical greenhouses may be a significant way forward for *ex situ* conservation. We look forward to hearing of others who have fallen under the spell of butterflies and plants. Once touched by the enchanter's wand, there can be no turning back.

Passiflora vitifolia *is a joy to behold, with or without butterflies.*

Further reading

Butterflies

Ackery, P. R. and Vane-Wright, R. I. (1984), *Milkweed Butterflies, Their Cladistics and Biology*. British Museum (Natural History), London, UK.
As well as a detailed discussion of the butterflies, this book also has an in-depth account of the larval foodplants and other relationships between danaids and plants.

Allan, P. B. M. (1979), *Larval Foodplants: A Vade-Mecum for the Field Lepidopterist*. Watkins and Doncaster, Kent, UK. (UK species only).
Many of the larval foodplants of UK species of butterflies and moths are listed in this small book but not those of any tropical species.

Carter, D. (1992), *Butterflies and Moths*. Eyewitness Handbook from Dorling Kindersley, London, UK.
Describes some of the enormous variation in adult butterfly and moth structure and appearance, with colour illustrations of preserved specimens and distribution for many tropical species.

De Vries, P. J. (1987), *The Butterflies of Costa Rica and Their Natural History*. Princeton University Press, USA.
This book contains virtually everything you need to know about many of the butterflies of Costa Rica, including lists of some of the natural foodplants of the species.

Emmel, T. C. (1976), *Butterflies*. Thames and Hudson, London, UK.
An absorbing and well-written book by a very eminent author that includes photographs of living butterflies and much useful information.

Goodden, R. (1971), *Butterflies*. Hamlyn, London, UK.
A small but well-written introductory book on the enormous subject of world butterflies, with many colour drawings.

Goodden, R. (1973), *All Colour Book of Butterflies*. Octopus, London, UK.
A short tour of the world's butterflies with large colour photographs, mostly of living specimens in their natural surroundings.

Goodden, R. (1977), *The Wonderful World of Butterflies and Moths*. Hamlyn, London, UK.
Another colour-illustrated book by one of the UK's leading experts.

Migdoll, I. (1988), *Field Guide to the Butterflies of Southern Africa*. New Holland, London, UK.
Much more than a colour-illustrated guide, with photographs of over 600 specimens and much useful biological information.

Preston-Mafham, R. and D. (1988), *Butterflies of the World*. Blandford, London, UK.
A fascinating book with some wonderful colour photographs of living butterflies.

Rothschild, M. and Farrell, C. (1983), *The Butterfly Gardener*. Michael Joseph and Rainbird, London, UK.
A most readable and informative book by two well-known experts that covers both the outdoor temperate butterfly garden and the greenhouse tropical one.

Rutowski, R. L. (1998), *Mating Strategies in Butterflies*. Scientific American, Vol. 279, No. 1, pp. 46-51. USA.
A short but interesting article that includes a discussion of the ultraviolet vision of butterflies and its role in mating.

Scoble, M. J. (1992), *The Lepidoptera, Form, Function and Diversity*. Natural History Museum Publications from Oxford University Press, Oxford, UK.
A very detailed account of the structure of butterflies for the specialist reader but with much interesting scientific information not easily available elsewhere.

Smart, P. (1975), *The Illustrated Encyclopedia of the Butterfly World*. Salamander, London.
Describes some of the enormous variation in adult butterfly structure and appearance, with chapters on general topics and hundreds of colour photographs, mostly of museum specimens.

Stanek, V. J. (1992 reprint, English translation), *The Illustrated Encyclopaedia of Butterflies and Moths*. Promotional Reprints, London.
Black-and-white and colour photographs, mostly of living specimens, with brief information on general biology and the species illustrated.

Stone, J. L. S. (1992), *Keeping and Breeding Butterflies and Other Exotica*. Blandford, London, UK.
This interesting book includes a chapter on the breeding of tropical butterflies but is mostly about temperate butterflies and other creatures.

Conservation

Barton, H. (1998), *A Safe Haven for Seeds*. Biologist, Vol. 45, No. 4 (September), pp. 151-154. London, UK.
A brief description of the Millennium Seed Bank that is being established at Wakehurst Place, West Sussex.

Blab, J. and Kudrna, O. (1982), *Aid Programme for Butterflies* (in German). Kilda Verlag, Germany.
Describes an eight-point plan for agriculture and land management which would help the conservation of butterflies outside of reserves.

Cherfas, J., Fanton, M. and Fanton, J. (1996), *The Seed Saver's Handbook*. Grower Books, Bristol, UK.
Gives detailed information on conserving plants outside of the major seed banks and why this is important.

Dunbar, D. (edit.) (1993), *Saving Butterflies: A Practical Guide to the Conservation of Butterflies*. Butterfly Conservation, Colchester, UK.
A useful guide to management of land for UK butterfly conservation.

Esko, E. (1996), *Healing Planet Earth: Macrobiotica and the New Ecology*. One Peaceful World Press, Becket, USA.
A thought-provoking small book on saving the world and all that's in it.

Feltwell, J. (1995), *The Conservation of Butterflies in Britain, Past and Present*. Wildlife Matters, East Sussex, UK.
A detailed discussion of general principles and problems, with specific examples, by a well-respected authority.

Fitter, R. (1986), *Wildlife for Man: How and Why We Should Conserve Our Species*. Collins, London, UK.
A wide-ranging and thorough discussion of the whole topic of conservation.

Hecht, S. and Cockburn, A. (1990), *The Fate of the Forest*. Penguin, Harmondsworth, UK.
An in-depth discussion of forest conservation worldwide.

Parsons, M. (1992), *Butterfly Farming and Tropical Forest Conservation in the Indo-Australia Region*. Supplement 1 to Tropical Lepidoptera, Vol. 3., Florida, USA.
Describes the role of human intervention to help conserve tropical butterflies by controlled breeding.

Plants

Brickell, C. (1996), *The RHS A–Z Encyclopedia of Garden Plants*. Dorling Kindersley, London, UK.
A useful source book for information on many plants commonly found in cultivation.

Herwig, R. (1989), *The Hamlyn Encyclopedia of House Plants*. Hamlyn, London, UK.
Contains information on some of the plants of interest to the tropical greenhouse gardener.

Heywood, V.H. (1978), *Flowering Plants of the World*. Oxford University Press, UK.
An excellent botanical overview of the world's flowering plant families.

Janzen, D. H. (1975), *Ecology of Plants in the Tropics*. Institute of Biology Studies in Biology No. 58, Edward Arnold, London, UK.
An introduction to the complexity of plant biology in tropical climates.

Pearce, E. A. and Smith, C. G. (1993), *The World Weather Guide*, 3rd edition. Helicon Pub., Oxford, UK.
A good introduction to data on all aspects of world weather.

Phillips, R. and Rix, M. (1997), *Conservatory and Indoor Plants*, Volume 2 (and Volume 1), Macmillan, London.
Useful reference books, with colour photographs of thousands of plants, many tropical.

Proctor, M., Yeo, P. and Lack, A. (1996, 2nd edition), *The Natural History of Pollination*. New Naturalist Series, HarperCollins, London, UK.
Looks in detail at the structure of flowers specially adapted for pollination by various agents.

Swithinbank, A. (1993), *The Conservatory Gardener*. Frances Lincoln, London, UK.
A useful source book for information on some of the plants of interest to the tropical greenhouse gardener.

Tampion, J. (1972), *The Gardener's Practical Botany*. David and Charles, Newton Abbot, UK.
A simple account of the principles of plant growth and factors that affect it.

Tampion, J. (1977), *Dangerous Plants*. David and Charles, Newton Abbot, UK.
An account of poisonous and allergenic plants, some of which may be grown in a tropical greenhouse.

Taylor, J. (1996), *Weather in the Garden*. John Murray, London, UK.
This gives a clear overview of the differences between an equatorial and a tropical climate as well as much other world climatic and vegetational information.

Vanderplank, J. (1996, 2nd edition), *Passion Flowers and Passion Fruit*. NCP, Clevedon, UK.
A fine introduction to the extremely complicated species and hybrids of the genus *Passiflora*. This book should be used to check the identification of any passion flowers that are bought because they often have the wrong names attached to them. It should certainly be consulted whenever heliconids are being bred.

Willis, J.C. (1973, 8th edition, revised by H.K. Airy Shaw), *A Dictionary of the Flowering Plants and Ferns*. Cambridge University Press, UK.
A source book to find the family of plants to which a genus belongs.

About the authors

Maureen and John Tampion were both born and educated in Southampton, where they were married in 1962. They have two adult sons. Maureen started her career in the book trade and then the law, while John followed a path leading to a degree in botany and a doctorate studying the date palm. While looking after the home and the children, and gardening on a variety of soil types, Maureen collaborated with John on many articles for gardening magazines, such as *Greenhouse Gardening* and *Amateur Gardening*, and books. John followed an academic career, teaching and researching at degree, doctorate and also post-doctorate level. For a number of years, they both carried out academic research on the micropropagation and tissue culture of plants while also developing their own tropical greenhouses. In 1990 they started their own butterflies picture library, agency and consultancy and concentrated on writing articles and books.

Index

DOLLS' HOUSES AND MINIATURES

CRAFTS

HOME & GARDENING

VIDEOS

Drop-in and Pinstuffed Seats	*David James*
Stuffover Upholstery	*David James*
Elliptical Turning	*David Springett*
Woodturning Wizardry	*David Springett*
Turning Between Centres: The Basics	*Dennis White*
Turning Bowls	*Dennis White*
Boxes, Goblets and Screw Threads	*Dennis White*
Novelties and Projects	*Dennis White*
Classic Profiles	*Dennis White*
Twists and Advanced Turning	*Dennis White*
Sharpening the Professional Way	*Jim Kingshott*
Sharpening Turning & Carving Tools	*Jim Kingshott*
Bowl Turning	*John Jordan*
Hollow Turning	*John Jordan*
Woodturning: A Foundation Course	*Keith Rowley*
Carving a Figure: The Female Form	*Ray Gonzalez*
The Router: A Beginner's Guide	*Alan Goodsell*
The Scroll Saw: A Beginner's Guide	*John Burke*

MAGAZINES

WOODTURNING

WOODCARVING

FURNITURE & CABINETMAKING

THE DOLLS' HOUSE MAGAZINE

CREATIVE CRAFTS FOR THE HOME

THE ROUTER

THE SCROLLSAW

BUSINESSMATTERS

The above represents a full list of all titles currently published or scheduled to be published.
All are available direct from the Publishers or through bookshops, newsagents and specialist retailers.
To place an order, or to obtain a complete catalogue, contact:

**GMC PUBLICATIONS, CASTLE PLACE,
166 HIGH STREET, LEWES,
EAST SUSSEX BN7 1XU
UNITED KINGDOM
TEL: 01273 488005 FAX: 01273 478606**

Orders by credit card are accepted